Praise for

TALENT

"I highly recommend this novel for anyone who loves theater or has ever sent a loved one to war."

—KATHLEEN M. RODGERS, author of the award-winning novel *Johnnie Come Lately*

"Goodwin has crafted the peer relationships, the parent, teacher, and other adult relationships with a layered depth and richness which I found both mesmerizing and uncommon."

—MARY JO DOIG, author of *Patchwork: A Memoir of Love and Loss*

"Bravo to B. Lynn Goodwin for a fast-paced, heartfelt story of love, loss, and finding your place in the world. Goodwin definitely writes teenagers well."

—RENEE ROBERSON, Editor of *CURRENTS* magazine

"From the deep desire for the freedom offered by a driver's license to the disappointment of trying out for something and not achieving a goal, Sandee shows the reader how to thrive under adversity. *Talent* is a page-flipping read!"

—JILL HEDGECOCK, author of *Between Shadow's Eyes* and *Rhino in the Room*

"The target reading group for this novel is high-schoolers. But don't let the age thing stop you; this book is for anyone who likes great writing and a powerful page turner."

—ANN M(CAULEY, author of *Runaway Grandma*

"Every reader will give Sandee Mason and identify with her journey of personal discovery and growth."

—ALINE SOULES, librarian and author of *Evening Sun* and *Meditation on Woman*

Talent

by B. Lynn Goodwin

© Copyright 2020 B. Lynn Goodwin

ISBN 978-1-64663-016-5

Published by

Köehlerbooks™

3705 Shore Drive
Virginia Beach, VA 23455
800–435–4811
www.koehlerbooks.com

Hope your Next Chapter Book Club will be interested.

TALENT

B. LYNN GOODWIN

Best wishes,

B. Lynn Goodwen-Brown

VIRGINIA BEACH
CAPE CHARLES

CHAPTER ONE

THIS IS THE DAY that could change my life.

I've been living in the shadow of my big brother, Brian Mason, all of my life, but in five more minutes, I'm going to audition for San Ramos High's spring production of *Oklahoma!* I'm reading for Ado Annie, who sings and dances and flirts, but if I don't get it, maybe I can play Gertie or Ellen or somebody else with lines.

Across the room, the ugly "Senior Sofa" is crammed with drama's elite in skinny jeans and faux fur jackets. They're hoping for leads too, and they're seniors. Where does that leave a sophomore like me? I slide my hand into my backpack and pull out two red M&Ms. The chocolate melts on my tongue and soothes my stomach.

Jenn McCall, the best singer in the sophomore class, slips in next to me, drops her backpack on the floor, and says, "How's your diet, Sandee?"

The scrawny twit speaks. Truthfully, she has an angelic voice inside her sexy body, but sometimes she acts like a diva. I'm about to tell her my diet's fine, but I never lie. Instead, I smile and say, "I gave it up. I'm a girl, not a stick."

"Okay, forget your figure. What's the chocolate doing to your vocal chords? You might as well wrap your instrument in cotton."

OMG! That's like hearing Bowen or some other teacher ask me why I'm sabotaging my future. So here's the whole truth: I eat when

I get nervous, and today I'm so nervous I grabbed a whole handful of M&Ms without even thinking.

We take auditions seriously here at San Ramos High. Once you're in the cast, you're part of the drama family. Our shows win awards. That's good for the college resume, but it goes deeper. We're all a part of one big show, and nobody ever treats a cast member like somebody's little sister.

Jenn leans over and whispers, "Want to warm up?" She's probably afraid to stretch alone. She cares what everyone thinks. I stopped caring seven months ago. I was too busy fighting my fears.

Mr. Jackson, the music teacher, takes his place at the piano. "On your feet, people," he says. His sturdy, dark fingers pound out the chords as we sing, "Mee may mi moe moo." I can't hear myself, so I touch my vocal chords. They're vibrating. My voice blends in perfectly, and I know I fit in here. I smile at Jenn as we sing, "Aluminum linoleum," up and down the scales. Then Mr. Jackson says, "They're ready, Ms. G." She's our director.

"Thanks, Mr. Jackson," she says like it's any ordinary day. "We'll continue with solos for Ado Annie. Jenn McCall, you're up." Ms. G taps her pen on her notepad the way she does when she's waiting for a scene to start in Beginning Drama.

Jenn wears a red skirt, a black turtleneck, and leather boots that fit like gloves. She slinks up the stairs, smiles at Ms. G, and says, "I'm ready."

Mr. Jackson pounds out the opening chords, and she sings, "I'm just a girl who cain't say no." I don't believe she means it, and that's pretty sad considering what a flirt she is.

"Nicole Lorca, you're next," Ms. G says after Jenn finishes the chorus.

Nicole sits next to the Senior Sofa, staring at the rings that sparkle on her fingers. She's new, I think, so when Jenn sits down I ask, "Do you know her?"

"She was Rizzo in *Grease* last spring."

"Rizzo had dark hair."

"She wore a wig, Sandee. Don't you know anything?"

"I know enough not to insult people when they make a mistake."

From the back of the room, Ms. G says, "Sandee, you're not making a favorable impression."

I clap my hand over my mouth and slowly turn. Her arms are folded across her chest, and she's giving me the same look she gives the kids who mouth off in class. She says, "Nicole, would you start again, please?"

Mr. Jackson plays the opening chords once more, and as Nicole starts the song over, Jenn whispers, "Great. Like she needs a second chance."

I don't know what to say, so I reach into my backpack for another M&M—just one.

Nicole's lilting voice fills the rehearsal room. It sparkles like the rings on her fingers.

My heart won't stop fluttering. Calm down and focus, I tell myself, just as Ms. G says the words that could change my life: "Sandee Mason, you're next."

I race up the stairs with my blood pulsing in my ears. A voice that sounds like my brother, Bri, whispers, "Go for it, Sandee." I want to turn around and look, but I know no one will be there.

Bri went missing in Afghanistan seven months ago.

CHAPTER TWO

SOMETIMES I HEAR BRI talking to me, from a little place in front of my right eye and an inch or two out from my scalp. Mostly he says, "It's going to be all right, Sandee."

The first time it happened, I asked, "How do you know?"

I think I heard him say, "Trust me," but maybe I imagined it.

This time he said, "Go for it, Sandee," which is a first. Whenever I hear Bri's voice, the knots in my stomach untangle. Even though I can't see him, I feel his support.

I walk to center stage, wishing I had a blow dryer for the palms of my hands. I turn to face the audience. They stare up at me. I stare back. I didn't know it would be this hard.

"Breathe, Sandee," Mr. Jackson says. He thinks I have stage fright. He has no clue.

I smile and say, "Right. I forgot. Breathe."

The audience laughs. Sometimes I get laughs without even trying. That's okay. *Oklahoma!* is a musical comedy.

I start laughing too, and we keep laughing together, louder and louder, until Ms. G says, "Okay, Sandee. Let's get on with it."

Mr. Jackson plays the same introductory chords he used for everyone.

Have fun. Flirt. Don't blow it. Those are my thoughts—not Bri's.

At exactly the right moment, I sing, "I'm just a girl who cain't say no," and Rob Cooper catches my eye. I haven't seen him since Bri went into the Army. Rob became Bri's best friend when they played on the same Little League team.

His old, goofy grin flashes across his face. Will he play Curley?

Over half of the audience watches, even though they heard the song yesterday and the day before. My smile is so big that it almost keeps me from articulating. I breathe in and sway to the music. This is fun. Adrenaline surges through me and lassos my nervousness. Kind of.

I belt out, "Just when I oughta say no," and cringe. My alto voice squeaks. Literally. Jenn puts her fingertips over her ears, and Ms. G scribbles something on her yellow pad. Ouch! I want a trapdoor to open up and swallow me.

"Thank you, Sandee," Ms. G says, in her neutral voice. I'm cut off. I slink back to my seat. Maybe I'll sell tickets or be an usher.

"Good try, Sandee," Jenn says as she crosses one knee over the other and tugs on her red skirt. "If you take Mixed Chorus, you'll get a lot of training for next year."

Across the room, Rob Cooper whispers something to the girl next to him. Is he reminding her that I'm the one whose brother went missing in Afghanistan? I hate not knowing.

I pick up my backpack and sneak down the row of chairs and out through the back of the rehearsal room, heading for the bathroom. I don't need to go. I need to get away from auditions. The tension is killing me.

The hinges squeak as I open the restroom door, and the sound reverberates against the porcelain tiles. Nicole stands in front of the sink, slurping mouthwash. When she hears the door squeak, her eyes widen. She spits a mouthful of blue stuff into the sink and caps her mouthwash bottle. Her hands shake as she shoves it into her backpack.

I pull out my hairbrush and say, "You really came to life onstage."

She giggles at herself in the mirror and says, "I'm just a girl who cain't say no." Then our eyes meet, and she adds, "At any rate, I used to be." I have no idea what she means. Before I can ask, she says, "Maybe you will be too, once you hear the truth about your brother."

That puzzles me. "The truth?"

"I don't know how you can keep it all together when you don't know . . . Aren't you afraid he might be . . . ?"

I can't stand the way she stumbles trying to tell me she thinks he's dead.

"I probably should keep my mouth shut, but you're a real trooper."

"Me? Why? You're the trooper. My friend just told me you played Rizzo in *Grease* when you were a sophomore. She is so jealous."

"Life was great that year. I had my whole life ahead of me."

"You still do," I say as she tucks her hairbrush into an overstuffed backpack. She walks out without answering me. I stare into the mirror over the sink. Doesn't she still have her whole life ahead of her? Bri's missing, not her.

A minty smell rises from the sink. Underneath it is a sour odor. I turn on the water to wash it away. Did she throw up right before I walked in?

When I return to the rehearsal room, someone new is singing. I stand in the doorway, staring at the small stage framed by a glossy charcoal wall that reflects the light. The windows on either side of the audience have grown dark. Someone should close the blinds.

I wait until the singer finishes to take my seat. No way I'm annoying Ms. G again.

At six o'clock she says, "A cast list will be posted before school tomorrow."

If only I hadn't gone off-key. I want to ask for a do-over, but that's not how auditions work. It's not how enemy fire works either. Bri is proof of that.

CHAPTER THREE

A CRESCENT MOON SHINES through the bare branches of the big oak outside the rehearsal room. I pull my coat tighter and watch my breath come out in frosty puffs as I walk out the door just in time to see Jenn get in a car with some juniors in a capella. I don't want to be her, but I'd love to borrow her velvety voice and have juniors offer me rides. Of course, in nine weeks and four days I'll have my own license, and maybe Dad will let me drive Bri's car until he comes home.

I'm halfway across the parking lot when I hear the familiar clomp of Diego's boots. Diego used to be my boyfriend back in seventh grade, and he's still a buddy. "How'd it go, Sanders?" he asks.

I'm glad he cares, but I'm not ready to tell him I blew it. I figure he'll hear about it from the band kids who hung out in the back of the room, so I say, "Fine, and don't call me Sanders."

"Can I walk with you?" This time he doesn't call me anything. The shirt inside his unzipped fleece jacket says *Chaotic Neutral*.

Wish he could neutralize the chaos in my life. I'm glad he's taking a stand on something. So much better than the seventh-grade Diego who used ketchup to fake an injury so he could get out of sixth and seventh periods. I told him to grow up. He didn't, so I told him we were through. He told me I was a snob. I told him I was being myself.

After about ten days, he said hello and so did I. We never talked about our fight, but we started talking about band and a history assignment that was a killer for both of us. We felt more comfortable when people stopped calling us a couple.

Today, I'm glad I'm not alone. I don't want to beat myself up about auditions. Doing that makes me crazy, and I can't control it any more than I can control how many M&Ms go in my mouth when I get nervous. I have to get out of my head, so I ask, "Why were you still at school?" as we cross the damp street.

"Detention."

"What'd you do this time?"

"Nothing."

I stare at him.

"It's what I didn't do," he says with a big, goofy grin.

Diego is so predictable. "Bowen got you for no math homework, right?"

He thrusts his chapped hands into his pockets and says, "I don't know how she expects us to do that crap when we don't get it. She did a couple of problems with me, and now I understand. Finally."

"Awesome."

"So what happened at auditions?"

"I went off-key." The silence gets so loud that I can hear the rhythm of our steps. In a choked voice I add, "I guess I won't be a singer." He still says nothing. I appreciate his giving me space. Of course, he could give me a little sympathy if he wanted to.

We turn down my street, which is three blocks from school. Older homes with deep porches and weathered wooden shingles placed far back behind lawns and trees with big, bare branches. "I'd invite you for dinner, but we have guests."

I'm lying, and he probably knows it. The truth is, I don't feel like having company. It's better to lie than to hurt him with the truth. He doesn't deserve that.

Last summer, when we got the news about Bri, Diego called and asked how he could help. No one else called for days, even though my Facebook friends kept talking about me as if I couldn't read their posts.

When September came, Diego walked me to school and stared right back at the kids who wouldn't stop gawking. He never said a word, but his glares made them turn away. It was a cool thing to do.

I don't want to talk about auditions or me, though, so I ask, "How's your band?" He plays keyboard and sometimes drums, and lately he's been composing. His band keeps switching between R&B, and oldies, and country. Maybe they're trying to find themselves, just like me.

"Good."

Big talker. I try again as we approach our houses. "Call me later. Maybe you can help me figure out math."

"Okay."

"Why don't you ever give me more than one-word answers?"

He shrugs. "Does it bother you? That's four words." He grins again. I giggle. I can't help it.

"Thanks for not bugging me about auditions."

He takes the mail out of the box, looks at it, and stuffs it back in. Dead leaves linger on the lawn even though it's January. "Why would I bug you?" he asks.

I reach out and touch his hand without thinking about it. "Those are a chapped mess. Put something on them, okay?"

"Sure, Mom."

"Shut up or I'll tell her you had detention again."

"Loser."

"Double loser," I call from the gate in the white fence that separates our yards and our worlds, but he's already closed the door.

CHAPTER FOUR

AFTER DINNER, I WALK through the living room, where Dad's staring at a basketball game. He doesn't see me.

I go upstairs and plop on my bed. One of the posters on my yellow wall says, *Follow your dream*, and another says, *My mess. My room. My business.*

I turn away, pick up my laptop, and start my homework. My eyes get heavy, but they pop right open when the phone buzzes. I click on a text from Ms. G and read, "We are sorry to inform you that . . ."

I stand at the edge of the stage pleading, "Let me try again, Ms. G. I can do it."

"No, Sandee. You had your chance. It's time to move on."

"Ple-e-e-ase."

I open my eyes. Light from the streetlamp comes through the mini blinds and makes stripes on the ceiling. I'm holding on to Spike's fur, and he's growling. Spike is eighty pounds of Dalmatian and love that Bri brought home six years ago. He took up sleeping with me after Bri left for the Army.

"Didn't mean to hurt you, Spike," I say as I loosen my grip.

His eyes say, "Apology accepted."

I check my iPhone. No text. No messages. No rejection. It was a dream.

Make that a nightmare. I can't believe I'm awake at 3:15 a.m. and my homework isn't done.

"Good dog," I say and stroke Spike's fur. "Do dogs dream?"

Of course, Spike can't answer. Sometimes he looks like he's running in his sleep, so maybe he dreams then.

"Let's get three more hours of shut-eye, Spike."

He settles his head between his paws. His eyes stay on me.

The next morning, a coat of frost covers the wooden benches outside the rehearsal room, and a typed list flutters on the bulletin board next to the door. "What's up with this?" one of the girls staring at it asks.

I lean in and read, "The following people should report to the rehearsal room immediately after seventh period." I skim past Lambert and Lincoln, and the next name is Mason. I read it again. Sandee Mason.

"I made it!" I scream. People press into me. "I really, really made it!"

"Chill, girl." It's not Bri's voice I hear this time. It's Diego's. He points at the list, where his name, Diego Rivera, is also written.

"You didn't even try out."

"I know. I signed up to play in the orchestra. I don't want to be onstage." I inch my way out of the crowd. He follows me, but we avoid eye contact.

"What part will you be playing?"

"Beats me. It's a list of names."

"How stupid! That's no cast list, and she knows it." I shake, standing in the frosty shadow of the big oak. How can Diego be on the list when he didn't try out?

We both hear the *tap-tap-tap* of Jenn's boots on the pebbled cement walkway.

"What did you get, Sandee?" she asks.

"Exactly the same thing you did. My name on a list."

"But—"

"Ms. G wrote, 'If your name is on the list, you're a part of the show.' I'm sure you're there too."

"There's more, but it fell on the ground." Nicole picks up a piece of paper and reads, "I need to look at a couple more people before I can tell you your parts. Please report to the rehearsal room right after seventh period."

The show isn't cast, but I'm a part of it—whatever that means.

Drama class meets after lunch. While the other kids take off coats and get scripts out of backpacks, I thunk my bag down next to my chair. My scene partner asks, "What's wrong?"

I explain about the list, and before I can tell her what I'm going to do, she says, "Ask Ms. G what it means." It's what Dad would tell me to do—or Bri, or even Mom.

"I know," I say, rolling my eyes.

I don't roll them in front of Ms. G, though. Instead, I ask, "Why are some people on the list when they weren't at auditions yesterday?" My voice trembles, and my stomach's in knots again.

"Who are you talking about?" Ms. G asks.

"Diego Rivera."

"He must have been one of Mr. Jackson's additions." She picks up her grade book, as if it's no big deal, and heads for the music stand she uses as a podium.

"Additions?" Additions and auditions sound a lot alike. Maybe I missed something.

"We didn't have enough boys try out, so I asked Mr. Jackson to recommend a few who could meet the time commitment and weren't essential for the orchestra. I'll bet Diego is one of those."

"That's not fair!" I hate it when good roles go to boys just because they're boys.

"Girls don't sound like cowboys, Sandee, and you're too curvy to look like one. Besides, we need the right blend of voices to make the music work."

Can he play it? He's no actor.

"I'm sure it doesn't seem fair," she says as if she read my mind, "but the show takes place back when Oklahoma was still a territory, and there's no other way to pull it off authentically. Cowgirls were an oddity back then. Besides, there are other jobs. It takes a huge team to put on a show, remember? Now, it's time to get class started."

I go back to my seat and hold my script in front of my face. No way I'll let anybody see the tears in my eyes. It's not my fault that I don't sing bass or tenor. I slide my hand into my pocket and sneak three M&Ms.

I sniff as I suck the chocolate and swirl it around in my mouth. Diego's my friend, and I want to be happy for him, but he's getting a role and he doesn't even want one.

At the callbacks after school, I sit next to Diego, who sits next to Jenn. "Good luck," I whisper, but my heart isn't in it.

"Thanks," he says before he turns to Jenn and asks, "Who is Ali Hakim?" like I know nothing about the script.

Boys!

After forty-five minutes of trying various actors together, Ms. G says, "Jenn, stay up and, Diego, please read the same scene with her."

My stomach is a volcano about to erupt. All I can do is watch the two of them. I see lust in Diego's eyes when he says, "Persian good-bye? Why, that ain't nuthin' compared to an Oklahoma hello!"

Jenn looks up at him like she's about to jump his bones.

He wraps his arms around her and leans in for the long kiss, but he looks stiff and awkward. Ms. G cuts them off, just as she's done with every other group.

I let out my breath. I didn't realize I'd been holding it. I can't believe Diego's about to soar ahead of me.

I grab a handful of M&Ms, but a second later, I drop them back in the bag. Candy can't solve this problem. Why is it a problem? Diego and I are just friends. He can do whatever he wants.

Diego follows Jenn off stage. He stares at her twitchy little butt. I remind myself he's only playing a role. I hope that's the truth.

CHAPTER FIVE

MS. G PROMISES THAT the complete cast list, with names and roles, will be posted on Monday morning. She says, "Enjoy your weekend," like that's possible when we don't know our parts. Outside, it can't be over forty degrees.

Diego, Jenn, and I are walking to my locker when Rob stops us. "I'm glad you're doing this, Sandee. Bri would be too."

I stare at the pebbled cement. I can't speak. When I look up, he smiles like he understands that I'm feeling awkward because Bri's missing. That's worse.

I'm so tired of being treated like a pity case because I'm Brian Mason's little sister. Sure, I miss him, but everybody treats me like a poster child for the sibling of the MIA soldier. I hate living in his shadow.

Rob says, "You three want to hang with the drama people tonight? We're watching the original *Dracula*. Lots of fake blood and overacting. It'll be ridiculous, but it's cool to see how we're already way better than the old-time professionals."

Jenn's body shifts inside her leather coat. "I'm working at the box office tonight." We all know that her parents now own the San Ramos Children's Theatre. Her grandmother started it, and she helps out. She likes living in the shadow of her family.

Rob cuts her off before she can launch into one of her I-am-important monologues. "We're just hanging out. It was supposed to be a casting celebration, but we can't do that without a cast list. Wanna come?"

Jenn flashes her flirty smile at Rob, who's almost six feet tall now. "Maybe someone can sub for me." Does she have a thing for Rob, or does she think flirting will help her get a role?

"Sandee?" Rob asks.

"Sorry, but I hate vampire stuff. It's not real and . . ." My throat muscles tighten. Every time someone mentions vampires or zombies or I hear about traffic fatalities or a shooting in Oakland, I think of Bri. What if he never makes it back? What if he's already—

I can't say it. Nobody says it, but everybody thinks it. I'm working on the show to stop obsessing about death. How is Dracula going to help that?

Rob interrupts my obsessive thoughts. "Okay, Sandee, but if you change your mind, you can still come, okay?"

"Sure."

"We can make fun of the Goth eyes and the ridiculous gestures." Diego's giving us his best John Wayne imitation, and his twinkling brown eyes bore into me.

"Great. See all three of you there. I've got to meet somebody," Rob says, and practically bolts towards the parking lot.

I'm not going, but I'm tired of saying so. Let Rob find out when I don't show up.

"He's a senior. Why would he want us at his party?" I ask Diego as we walk to my locker. The wind whips around us, and a clump of oak leaves and baby acorns thunk onto the grass beside me.

Before Diego can answer, Jenn says, "He does it to encourage us to be an ensemble. Go, Sandee. If you hate the blood and gore, ignore the movie. You've got something in common with the upperclassmen this weekend."

Streetlights swoop in and out of the car windows as Diego's dad drives all three of us to the party that night. Mr. Rivera invites me to sit in the passenger seat. Diego sits in back with Jenn. Her dad's running the box office this one time.

In two months and twenty-eight days, I'll go to the DMV and walk out a licensed driver. I can't wait until I don't have to ask for rides. Of course, I won't be allowed to drive anyone under eighteen after dark for a year. I hate that rule. They force us to be careful; they say it saves lives. Then we turn eighteen, and a lot of kids join the Army and go missing or get shot.

"You okay, Sandee?" Diego asks.

I nod, but I don't speak. A surge of panic mixes with the same nervousness that almost overwhelmed me at auditions. I listen for Bri's encouragement, but I don't hear it.

Diego's dad pulls up to the curb and lets us off. Rob's house stands on top of a sloped lawn. The porch light is on, and even from the street, we can see the big screen flashing MTV videos into the darkened living room. Clusters of drama kids wear grunge, funk, and casual chic. I stand on one side of the front door and Jenn stands on the other as Diego rings the bell.

"Come in," someone calls over the horror music thrumming behind the door.

Rob sees us across the room and shouts, "Glad you made it. Movie will start in ten. Want a beer?"

My chest tightens. I haven't been to a party in months, much less a party with seniors. I don't drink, and I don't need the extra calories in beer. I look around. Some kids hold soft drinks. "Maybe later," I say with a confidence I don't feel.

"I'll try one," Diego says, and his eyes gleam as if he were a vampire about to bite into a trembling neck. Does he realize he told everyone he's never had a drink before by saying, "I'll try one"?

"You, Jenn?" Rob asks.

"Maybe later with Sandee. I'll have a diet soda if you've got any."

"Got any bottled water?" I ask.

"Good choice, Sandee. I'll take one too," Jenn purrs.

Rob brings us our drinks and turns off the horror music. Somebody dims the lights. Thespians, choir people, and band members all point their chairs towards the big-screen TV. Jenn perches on the edge of Diego's armchair. They probably think they look cozy. There's a cushion in the window seat where I can see the audience better than the screen. I sit there. I love watching the audience's reactions.

Five kids squeeze themselves onto a sofa big enough for three. Nicole, the girl with the sparkly rings who sang so beautifully, sits on the end, clutching a bottle of water. If I'd brought my camera I'd capture her isolation in the midst of a crowd—the flowing auburn hair and the tightly clutched hands, the animation of the other kids against her stillness. Like I said, I love watching audiences. I took photos all the time before Bri disappeared.

Rob says, "Move over," and sits next to me. "Want that beer now?" He takes a slurp off the top before he hands it to me. I set it at my feet. He slides his arm behind me. "I'm glad you're here, Sandee. Drama's going to open up a whole new world to you."

"Do you know something about the cast list?" He doesn't answer. "Do you know who I'm playing?" I don't think Ms. G would consult him, but anything's possible.

"Calm down. You're not going to find out till Monday. Suspense is part of the theater ritual."

I hate it when people keep secrets.

"Aren't you going to try your beer?" he asks.

"Do you know?" I ignore the beer.

"You're persistent," he says, and his grin is irresistible.

"Just for the record, you're impossible," I say. I pick up my untouched beer and wiggle it in his face.

His fingertips knead my shoulders. "Relax. The beer will help."

"Whatever." I take a sip. It's bubbly, and its coldness reminds me of fall and orange leaves and football games. Curiously, I sip again. I don't feel any buzz. Why is beer such a big deal? The bubbles just dance against my insides. On my third swallow, I taste the bitterness I've heard boys talking about. Rob keeps rubbing my shoulders.

A boy I do not know comes by, thrusts a bowl of chips in our faces, and says, "Take your hands off her and eat some chips, Big Man."

"Big Man?" I ask.

He ignores me. "Sandee, this is Dwight. He graduated last spring, but he keeps hanging around."

"I'm in drama at Pine Mountain College now, and I came to Rob's party to check out all the foxy chicks. You're new."

"She's Brian Mason's little sister," Rob says, "and she auditioned for *Oklahoma!*"

"Well, good luck, little lady." He sounds like another bad John Wayne imitation. "Big Man here is a great connection to the San Ramos drama department."

"Thanks." My head is back on "foxy chicks." Nobody's ever called me foxy before. I can't stop smiling, and my insides glow for the first time in a long time.

After Dwight leaves, Rob leans in and whispers, "I think he likes you, but he's not your type."

"How do you know my type?"

He grins.

I take another sip of my beer because his silence makes me uncomfortable. "I'll watch the movie now, okay? It's way different than I thought it'd be. The vampires aren't anything like dead people."

"Okay, sugar," he says. At least that's what I think he says. But why is Rob calling me sugar—or did I mishear?

Jenn told me that Rob and Nicole were a big item last year. I look over at Rob, wanting to ask who broke up with whom, but it takes too much effort to form the words. My muscles relax, and Rob's arm is a comfortable weight on my shoulder. I haven't felt this good since we learned that Bri was MIA.

I take one more sip of beer—a long, slow, deep one. It tickles as it goes down, but it warms me. It's every bit as soothing as chocolate.

CHAPTER SIX

WHEN I WALK INTO the rehearsal room before the first read-through, Ms. G sits at her desk next to the door. She marks *90%* on the top of a paper and flips it over.

"Assistant stage manager reporting for duty. What do you want me to do?"

She looks up and caps her pen. "Right now, get started on your geometry homework. I shared the cast list with the teachers. That includes your geometry teacher."

I don't say Bowen is a dinosaur in polyester and Nikes—as much as I want to. Nor do I say she thinks the entire world lives and breathes math. Instead, I sit down and try to start my homework. Too bad I can't concentrate with all the chatter and excitement generated by the actors.

Diego plops down beside me and asks, "Where's Jenn?"

"Probably in the restroom getting gorgeous. She does it all with makeup, you know."

He glares, until I say, "What?"

"This is new. When did you get rude?"

I stare at my book. He pulls his arms out of the North Face jacket he got for Christmas. I can't stop looking at the way his T-shirt hugs his chest, which is so stupid. We haven't been boyfriend and girlfriend since the seventh grade. Even so, I want to protect him from Jenn. She uses guys.

Ms. G stands behind the music stand and says, "Settle down, folks." Six seniors cram onto the ugly green sofa on the far side of the room, while others open folding metal chairs or stand next to the walls. A sign over the door says, *Capacity 60*. Eighty-nine members of the cast and crew breathe as if we are one excited body.

"First of all I want to congratulate everyone. We saw some very talented people at auditions, and Mr. Jackson and I feel we have an excellent cast."

A creaking door interrupts her, and a strip of sunlight reflects off the polished, mahogany piano. Everyone turns as the strip widens. Rob, Nicole, and Jenn file in, a little like a platoon in formation.

"Of course no one is irreplaceable," Ms. G says, staring straight at them.

Busted.

The last three folding chairs clang together as Rob fumbles with them. "Sorry we're late, Ms. G. One-shot deal."

Instead of answering him, she says, "Sandee, will you pass out the paperwork? Rob, give her a hand."

He shoves the last chair out of the way, grabs the stack of scripts, and leaves me with the co-curricular contracts.

"Mr. Jackson and I will treat you like professional actors as long as you come to rehearsals on time, keep a B average, follow school rules, and honor the zero-tolerance policy with regard to drug and alcohol use." I cringe when she mentions the B average. I do well in English and computers and okay in history and Spanish, but I have C-minuses in Beginning Geometry and Earth Science.

"As you read, think about what your character wants. Rob, will you start us off with the stage directions at the top of Act One, Scene One?" Ms. G asks.

It's really happening. We're starting the rehearsal, and I'm not in the cast.

Rob reads with a rich baritone, but he slurs. She should have asked me to read. By the time we get to the second scene, I've opened a fresh pack of M&Ms, which are still stashed in the left pocket of my corduroy jacket. I didn't buy any today, and I hope I won't tomorrow, but I don't want to waste the ones I have.

I slide my hand into the package, slide three out, and sneak them into my mouth, one at a time. While everyone's looking at the script, I suck on the chocolate. My eating is no worse than their reading. *Is this the talented cast Ms. G talked about?*

She calls a ten-minute break between Acts One and Two. Actors and designers crowd around her with questions. She sees me at the back of the crowd, holds out a stack of audition forms and says, "Please alphabetize these and give them to Rob so he can make a call sheet, and put the M&Ms away. You know there's no eating in here."

My cheeks burn. I grab the sheets and turn away, while an actor with an open calendar asks, "What days does Will Parker have to be here?" How can she not realize she's embarrassed me?

Rob calls the cast back for the second act, his resonant voice echoing across the courtyard. I sit down with the stack of eighty-nine contact sheets that Ms. G collected before auditions. Alphabetizing is better than listening, and I find out where Nicole and the other leads live—not that I plan to become the San Ramos High Stalker.

Jenn and Diego sit with Nicole and the other actors after the break. Rob has moved up and sits next to Ms. G. He looks pretty foxy. Like Diego, he's wearing a new North Face jacket, and it matches his chocolate eyes. Maybe the fact that his jacket matches his eyes is a coincidence, but some guys have egos that won't quit.

The sky has darkened to sapphire, and the forms are in alphabetical order when Ms. G says, "Call for tomorrow is Act One, Scene One promptly at three." She glares at Rob as she says "promptly." The cast is already gathering up backpacks and putting on jackets and gloves. Rob salutes.

Ms. G doesn't see it. She calls out, "If anyone knows where we can rent or borrow the surrey with the fringe on top, please let me know" as we pour out of the theater, texting or jangling car keys.

"Want to walk with me, Sandee?" Jenn asks.

Since when do we live near each other? "I have to give these to Rob first," I say, holding up the stack of papers.

"Try backstage. He used to close up back there after *Harvey* rehearsals."

He isn't there, though. Ms. G spots me coming offstage and says, "Did you forget to give those call sheets to Rob?"

"I can't find him."

"He'll be with the leads outside."

They're all gathered next to a weathered bench. It has a plaque on the back that says *From the Class of '67.* It stands under a live oak that was around when the land belonged to the Ohlone Indians.

"Rob?"

No answer. What am I? Invisible? "Rob?" I say louder.

The girl playing Laurey points at me, and I feel like I did back in the fall when school started and everyone treated me differently because Bri was missing. "Hi, Sandee. Do you need something?" she asks.

"I think Rob needs something." I thrust the papers into his hands. "Ms. G said you're supposed to—"

"Make a call sheet," everyone says in unison. "We've done this before, Sandee."

"Okay. . . "

"Relax, kiddo." Rob's voice is gentle. "You're doing fine. See you tomorrow."

Kiddo? Really? I'm not eleven.

I turn to go and hear someone laugh. I don't look back. Diego's standing at the edge of the parking lot with Jenn, and we all walk up Sycamore Lane together. I smell the newly cut wood on the frames of the condos going up. Jenn's father pulls up and offers us all a ride, but Diego and I say no. Instead, we cross the empty lot beside the new condos and come out on our street, which has low ranch houses with deep porches and old sycamores along the sidewalk.

When we get to Diego's house, he puts his hand on the gate, but he doesn't open it. "I'm sorry you didn't get a part. I felt so awful sitting there today, knowing you're the actor."

"Old musicals have more parts for guys. I'm a girl, and you're a guy, and there's nothing we can do about that." My face grows hot, and my ears burn. A broad grin spreads across his face, and we both burst out laughing.

"So you're not jealous?"

"Not about your role." I bite my lip. I don't want him to think I'm jealous because he's onstage with Jenn. "You know what I mean. I thought being assistant stage manager was better than being on crew, but so far I feel like a peon."

"You're no peon," he says, and his eyes sparkle like they did when he flirted with Jenn during the audition.

I have no idea what to say, so I ask, "Do you think it would be okay to ask Ms. G for more responsibility?"

"Are you kidding me?"

"No. I want to do more." I could go on, but my heart starts beating against my ribs.

"Go for it if you want to, but it sounds silly to me."

Maybe Diego doesn't get me after all. How can he not know that my parents are still hung up on Bri when I'm the one who's here?

Why do I care what Diego thinks? We stopped being boyfriend and girlfriend in the seventh grade.

CHAPTER SEVEN

DIEGO STANDS AT THE edge of the stage and says, "May I have a suggestion of an activity you could do in front of your grandmother?"

"Bowling," someone in the darkened class calls out.

This is odd. Diego isn't in drama.

"Carving a turkey."

"Shining your shoes," someone says over the carving-a-turkey remark.

"I heard bowling first. Thank you."

I step forward. "May I have a suggestion of a place?"

"In a graveyard."

"In a war zone. Oops. Sorry."

Ms. G says, "People, please!"

"I heard graveyard first. We're going to be bowling in a graveyard."

The audience laughs. Diego looks lost. So I roll an imaginary bowling ball into an imaginary headstone, turn to Diego, and say, "Do we count that as a strike or a spare?"

"I don't know."

"Of course you do. It was your idea to cut seventh period and come here."

"To drama class?"

"No, silly. To the graveyard."

"Why are we bowling *here*?"

"Don't you remember saying, 'It'll be a prank everyone will talk about for years?'"

He stares.

"Sammy," I say, because I'm talking to his character and not him, "what's happened to your mind?"

"I left it in my locker?" A few people laugh.

I sit on my knees and pull the weeds growing by the base of the imaginary tombstone. "Stuart McMasters," I read from a gravestone that only I can see. "I wonder how he died. I wonder who he was. Who do you think he was?"

"Maybe he was the first McMasters in San Ramos. Maybe he had the dry goods store. The stone says 'Born 1884. Died 1914.'" Diego is reading his own version of the imaginary gravestone. This is good. He's becoming Sammy.

"Maybe he was a soldier who died in the war and they shipped his body home and his family buried him here."

Diego looks confused, and he's Diego again—not Sammy.

"Put the bowling ball back in the bag and help me clean up his grave, okay?" My voice cracks.

"Yeah, it's a mess. Nobody takes care of it. Probably his whole family is dead."

I look down at the imaginary weeds and into the imaginary bag where I'm putting them. I look into the wings of our little stage in the rehearsal room.

Real tears fill my eyes—the kind I cried when Bri went missing. I don't think I could stop crying even if the scene stopped right then.

"Do you think the dead realize they're lying in cemeteries, Sammy?" I ask through my tears.

Out of nowhere, I hear my father's early morning clump on the Persian rug outside my bedroom. He's bringing Mom her first cup of coffee.

I struggle to open my eyelids. Sun streams in through the cracks in the mini blinds. Diego and the graveyard fade.

My heart pounds as I call through the door, "Dad, is Bri okay?"

He opens my door and gives me a funny look. I rub my eyes. "Oh, honey, have you been dreaming? He disappeared in Afghanistan, remember?"

I look away. He closes the door softly. He always does that. Practical dad, the Army captain, can't stand tears. Our family doesn't cry together. Silence is easier. My parents have no idea how often I cry alone.

On the way to school, I tell Diego about my dream. "What's an improv?" he asks.

I explain it's a scene we make up after getting a suggestion of an activity from the audience.

"You mean you get a suggestion and go off and plan it?"

"No, we get a suggestion and just start. We trust each other."

He gives me a look that says, "You've got to be kidding."

"Okay. It's a little more complicated than that, but you and I were doing an unscripted scene in my drama class."

"The only acting I've done lately is getting out of homework, and that's more lying than acting."

"There's your role as Cord Elam." I can't believe I said it. He'll think I'm guilt-tripping him, and I'm not. I press my lips together, and we walk on in silence.

Our breath makes frost clouds that swirl into one another and disappear. "Why do you like this drama stuff so much?" he finally asks.

"You'll find out when we get to opening night. We've only been rehearsing for two weeks. " I breathe in deeply, trying to calm myself. All I've done in two weeks is alphabetize the contact sheets, make a few phone calls for Ms. G, and write down blocking the day Rob was out with the flu.

Spring semester starts today. I still have Bowen, but my English teacher, Mrs. Marron, a tiny woman with a big voice who constantly moves her hands, is new. She used to be a sub. Ms. Litke, my old English teacher, introduced her on Friday. Ms. L's husband was transferred to Chicago. If Mrs. Marron asks us to introduce ourselves, I'll say I'm Sandee, the assistant stage manager of *Oklahoma!*, and ask if she ever did theater in high school and what it was like for her.

After school, Jenn sits down at the piano in the rehearsal room and plays a song from *Glee*. A bunch of kids sing along, making up new words.

Ms. G sits alone at her desk. The perfect time to get an answer. I walk over and ask, "What exactly is an assistant stage manager supposed to do?" My palms sweat almost as much as they did during auditions.

"You're doing fine," she says, without looking up from the papers she's grading.

"I'd like to do more. I'm kind of bored sitting around at rehearsals."

She raises her eyebrows the way she did when I talked too much during auditions.

"I don't mean to be offensive. I just think I could do more."

"Okay, Sandee. Bethany was props mistress, but she quit after finals. Would you like to take her job on?"

"Would I still be the ASM?" I ask over all the actors who are now singing "Superman."

"Do you think you can handle both jobs?"

"Of course."

"That's what I like to hear. When we don't need you at rehearsal, you can be out collecting props." She hands me a script and says, "Go to the office and ask Ms. Tarmash to make a copy of the props list and charge it to drama. Then look in the cabinets, see what we already have, and bring me a list tomorrow, okay?"

"Absolutely."

"We need 1905 styles, but we don't want anything that looks used or tattered."

"I'm on it." I love saying those words.

I'm in such a hurry that I run into Rob. Literally.

"Where are you going, kiddo?" he asks as he reaches for the script I dropped on the pebbled cement. I hate *kiddo* even more than Sanders.

"To make copies of the props list, Big Man."

"Don't call me that," he snaps.

"Then don't call me kiddo, okay? I'm making a copy of the props list because I'm replacing Bethany." I love my new confidence.

"Whatever," he says. He takes his jacket off, and his tight red T-shirt says *Coke* on the front. "You're going to be one busy lady. Hope you can handle it all."

"Of course I can," I say as I step around him. "It's not like I'm doing anything as ASM."

"Just wait," he said, but I'm through waiting. Today I'll contribute. Props mistress and ASM. None of the actors has two jobs. *Oklahoma!* is going to be awesome.

CHAPTER EIGHT

WE'RE BLOCKING ACT ONE. Rob writes notes for everyone in the prompt book, and most of the actors also write the directions in their scripts, while I sit in the back trying to do the last geometry proof. I look up when I hear Mr. Jackson say, "Everybody except Curly and Laurey, take ten." He beckons to the two of them, and they look at each other and laugh nervously. They both know they were off-key.

While they stand by the piano, reworking each phrase, Ms. G spots me sitting in the back row. I hold up my geometry book so she'll know I'm doing my homework, but that's not her concern. "How are the props coming along, Sandee?" she asks as the leads sing "People Will Say We're in Love."

"I've brought in the easy ones, but some things don't even exist. How are we going to get a coal hod?"

"Well, you could—"

Before she can finish her statement, I get a fabulous idea. "How would you feel about our using some authentic antiques in the show?"

Her forehead crinkles, the way it does when she's about to say "Are you sure?" but this time she asks, "What do you have in mind?"

"My mom's the manager at Generation to Generation. I'll bet they'd be willing to lend us stuff, unless you think antiques look too old and battered."

Mom has been depressed since Bri disappeared. Dad suggested she quit working. Her boss, Alicia, offered her a leave, but two weeks later, she went back. She was going stir crazy without something to do all day. If she and I go through the props list together and she lets me borrow stuff, maybe Mom and I can have a real conversation that has nothing to do with Bri.

"It would be great to have your mom involved." Ms. G says, "Would she like to join Drama Boosters?"

I shrug. My throat closes up as I think of the big what if: What if Bri doesn't come back? That thought pops up at the weirdest times. Everybody wants things back to normal, but how can they be when every phone call could bring the best or worst news in the world?

"I'll ask her today if you don't need me here."

"Go, Sandee. It's a good idea."

I need a way to get everything back to the theater, so I beckon to Rob and ask, "Can you pick me up if I need to haul some props back here?"

"Text me so you don't interrupt rehearsal."

Outside I see Diego talking to Jenn. "Good luck in rehearsal," I say as I pass him outside the theater. I keep the "good luck" general, even though he needs it and she doesn't. Playing an old man does not come easily to him.

"At least I'm not going off-key," he says with a big, goofy grin.

My whole life went off-key when Bri went missing.

The clapper jingles as I open the arched doors of Generation to Generation. High ceilings swallow up the sound of the little clapper. Walking on the wooden floor, I imagine Oklahoma City back in the early 1900s.

The curio cabinets smell musty, even though Mom's always dusting everything. I look through the glass at silver dishes, tobacco pouches, and cut glass. Once, they were family treasures. Emeralds, rubies, and sapphires glimmer on tarnished brooches. So sad to see wedding rings sitting next to them. We'll never have to sell our valuables as long as Dad has his Army pension, but money can't help us find Bri. Did he give away something more precious than family heirlooms when he joined the Army? Dad said he went of his own free will, but no one expected him to pay this high a price.

I hear Mom's professional voice, soft and engaging, and see the cell phone next to her ear. She stands beside shelves filled with copper teapots, coffee grinders, and old Schilling tins labeled sage, cayenne, and allspice.

"We'll look forward to seeing you on Friday," Mom says. She spots me hanging out near the entrance and asks, "Why aren't you at rehearsal?" with more urgency than I've heard in months.

"I told you I'm doing props, right?"

"What does that have to do with your visit, sweetie?"

"Can you lend the show some things from the early 1900s?" I didn't mean to blurt it out. Why is it so hard to talk to my own mother?

I give her a copy of the props list. "Is this a coal hod?" I ask, pointing to a black thing that almost sent me sprawling when I walked in.

"I didn't know you'd ever heard of such a thing." She smiles like she's proud of me. "Sweetie, you need to understand that Alicia decides what we lend, not me. Why don't you make something out of tin and paint it or borrow one from a hardware store?"

"We'll give you guys credit in the program. Think of the publicity," I say as if I haven't heard her. She starts straightening the shelves, which are already in perfect order. She won't look at me. "Mom?"

The little feathers on her duster flap. "I'm the manager, not the owner. You know that."

"I'll bet we could give the store a free ad." She keeps fluttering the stupid duster around, but she doesn't say anything. I take it out of her hands as if she were a child and say, "Mom, why can't you look at me?"

"I told you, I don't have the authority to loan these things."

"Take initiative. Ask Alicia. She'd be proud of you, and so would I."

"Sweetie, I have enough on my mind."

I pick up my backpack and say, "Sorry." Nothing more. Halfway across the store, I turn around, though. "Why do I have a mother who shuts me out? Everybody keeps telling me that life goes on. I wish you could support me half as much as you supported Bri when he got involved in Student Council."

Her eyes shine too brightly, and I'm afraid she's going to cry. "I can't talk about this here," she whispers.

"Okay," I say, though it's far from okay.

"Can we talk about it tonight, when I get home?"

"Whatever." I pick up a tag that's lying on the wooden floor and hand it to her.

"Don't go. Let me look at your list and see if you need anything that's been here over a year. Alicia loans inventory that won't move." She's tense, but she's trying.

I give her the list. Her hands shake as she puts on her glasses, but two minutes later, her shoulders relax. She goes to the computer to check the inventory. She's okay as long as she has something to do. Guess it runs in the family. She grabs a shopping basket and fills it with a smelling salts bottle, a small carpet beater, and a child's kaleidoscope that could pass for the "Little Wonder." She does it all without saying a word.

"Thanks, Mom." I stash the pieces into a canvas duffel bag.

"We've got an old wicker rocking chair in the back, but it's got some holes."

"Show me. We can cover holes with a quilt or pillows, and I don't think anybody sits in it."

I like it so much that Mom shows me some old crates and stools that Alicia plans to throw away. With paint and varnish we can make them look like they've sat on Aunt Eller's porch for years. There's even a narrow barrel that we can turn into a butter churn.

"This is awesome, Mom," I say as she helps me carry my stash out to the sidewalk. "Thank you soooo much! Want to join the Drama Boosters?"

She smiles sadly. "You always want more, just like your dad."

"Is that bad?"

"I'll think about it," she says. I figure that means no, but at least I tried.

"Thanks again, Mom," I say as we wait amidst the blue shadows of the buildings.

She doesn't say anything. Maybe she doesn't want my thanks.

"You know I didn't mean to yell at you earlier, don't you?" I'm not sorry I said it, but I didn't mean to crush her with it.

She puts her manicured fingers on my arm. "Your father and I never mean to cut you out." Her voice quavers. She won't look at me. Maybe she can't.

The cold winter sun is about to slip behind the ridge, and I'm about to hug her when Rob's red Honda CRV turns the corner.

"I probably need to get back inside," she says as soon as she sees it.

She knows Rob, of course, but saying hello would lead to a conversation about Bri. We're into our eighth month, and she's still not ready to talk about him.

Rob's quiet as he tries to get the rocker in his trunk, but no matter how he twists and turns it, the lid won't close.

"Can you tie the trunk down?" I ask.

"Grab the rope in the backseat?" Rob loops and knots the rope, while I hold the rocker steady. We put the other props in the back seat, and I climb in front. He chews his lip as he drives. I want to know why, but I can't ask what he's obsessing about. He'd never tell his troubles to Bri's kid sister.

"Is Ms. G waiting for us?" I finally ask. It's a lame question, but the silence is killing me.

"She had to go, but she gave me a note for the night custodian. He'll open up and lock it again."

"Wow. I'll bet 95 percent of the school doesn't know you can do that."

He smiles and says, "Life is full of surprises, kiddo." Then he winks.

I ignore the wink and say, "I asked you not to call me that, remember?" Maybe the direct approach will help him see how mature I've become.

Rob says, "I've called you that since Bri and I played Little League. We used to watch you and Diego hiding in the tree house, and one day we sat next to the window, smoking, just to see what you'd do."

"I remember. Diego was afraid you'd set the place on fire."

"I'd almost forgotten that." He swings into the school. He pulls up next to the rehearsal room, hands me his keys, and says, "See if you can untie that thing while I find the janitor."

After I loosen the rocker, I sit behind the wheel and put the keys back in the ignition. I don't expect Rob to let me drive home, but I love the fantasy.

Rob comes back with the custodian, Paul, who has a round belly under his gray uniform and a receding hairline. While he hauls the rocker inside, Rob opens the door and says, "Out."

"I'm not doing anything."

"You're not going to, either. Give me my keys."

"Fine. Whatever. I know how to drive. I'm just waiting for my birthday to get my license."

"News flash: My insurance doesn't cover unlicensed drivers."

"Okay." I yank the keys out of the ignition, but I don't want him to think I'm upset, so I calmly hand them to him and say, "It never hurts to try," as sweetly as I can.

Instead of being impressed, he starts lecturing. "Once you get your license you either play by the rules or pay the price. I'm not winding up like. . . "

"Like who?"

"Let's get this stuff inside," he says in a voice that warns me to shut up.

Everything except the rocker goes in the props cabinet. Good thing he knows the combination. The custodian, who has been watching us feud over driving rights, follows us out, shaking his head, and locks the door behind us. As soon as he's out of sight, Rob says, "You did good today. Want a ride home?" Does he even remember that I was sitting in the driver's seat with the key in the ignition?

"Absolutely." I'm getting a ride home with a senior. After we pull out of the parking lot I say, "Is this show going to be easier than *Harvey*?"

He scowls at the windshield. I hate his emotional roller coaster. "What do you know about *Harvey*?"

"I know Jenn worked props and you two didn't get along." His veins bulge. "What happened?"

"I yelled at her because she wasn't doing her job. She's used to being a queen bee, and she took it personally." He pulls onto my tree-lined street. The shadows of the leaves dance under the streetlights.

"Why is she still so pissed?"

"Don't quote me, but that chick seriously needs an attitude adjustment. I know she might be a prima donna down at the children's theater, but that doesn't carry any weight here."

"Can you tell me why Nicole wasn't in *Harvey*?" I ask, as he parks in front of my house. I figure, why not ask, since we are on a roll.

"Ask Nicole. Frankly, I'm surprised she's even back here, but this school loves to give people second chances."

"Second chances?"

"Is there an echo in here?"

"Answer me."

"Sandee, get out of the car," he says, and he leans across me to open the door. His hand brushes my breast through my corduroy jacket. I look at him, but he's digging through his CDs. Does he think I'm that naïve?

CHAPTER NINE

WHEN I WALK INSIDE our house after Rob cops a feel, I hear pots and pans clattering.

Our kitchen smells both luscious and lived in. Mom's cooking for the first time in months. "What's for dinner?" I ask as I walk into the kitchen.

"Turkey meatloaf. Salad. Broccoli without cheese." I know she worries about my weight, but I miss the au gratin potatoes and the chocolate cake she used to make for Bri and his friends.

"Rob loves the props."

She goes right on as if I haven't said anything. "I'm so sorry to do this to you, sweetie, but I'm going to a Blue Star Moms meeting tonight." Blue Star Moms is the place where moms of service men and women go to talk, commiserate, and send packages to servicemen.

"That's great! You haven't been since Bri went missing."

"What you said at the shop made me realize I'm acting as if he's dead. He's not. . . "

I wiggle out of my coat. "How do you know he's not?"

"The Army would have told us."

My face is hot, and my voice trembles as I say, "The Army can't find him, remember?"

Mom takes me in her arms and says, "Sweetie, there's nothing we can do about it. That's why I'm going to Blue Star Moms. You did a good thing agreeing to collect props when you didn't get a part, and I'm proud of you, but it's taking me a little more time to move on. I'm sure Bri is proud of you."

She's still hugging me when I say, "This is going to sound weird, but sometimes I hear him encouraging me."

She strokes my hair. "I keep replaying our conversations in my head too."

This is different. I'm not replaying conversations. At auditions I know I heard him tell me to go for it while I climbed the stairs. Mom will say I'm losing it if I tell her. She'll send me back to the grief counselor, who'll stare at me and ask, "How does that make you feel?"

"Your dad should be here any minute. Can you finish getting dinner ready?" Our conversation slides away like a dream.

"Instructions?" I ask, even though I know the drill.

"The veggies will be ready in five minutes. Drain them. Take the meatloaf out of the oven when the buzzer rings, and you and your dad can have dinner together, just the two of you."

That used to be a treat, back when Bri and I were competing to be the number one child. Now it doesn't matter.

She grabs the handbag she's thrown on the stepstool near the back door, pulls on her quilted maroon coat and a knit hat that looks like a rainbow, and dashes out.

I could start my homework, but I rarely have the house to myself. I turn on the TV, put in a *Glee* DVD, and sing and dance with the cast from last season. I'm standing on the coffee table, singing into my hairbrush, when Dad calls out, "Something burning, Susan?"

The veggies. I jump down, but Dad's already pouring water into the pan.

Steam rises, and I know the bottom is blackened. "I didn't hear the buzzer."

"Where's your mom?" he asks, as if I haven't said anything.

"You're not going to believe this, Dad. She went to a Blue Star Moms meeting."

"Thank goodness," he mutters as he digs at the burned broccoli. "What do you say we skip this? I smell meatloaf and that's enough for me if you make me a little garlic bread to go with it."

"Sure. We've got salad too." I get out the butter and garlic while he stuffs the charred broccoli down the disposal.

We're almost finished eating when I ask, "Dad, do you know anything about Nicole Lorca's family?"

After retiring from the Army, Dad went to work for Grayco Insurance. He likes helping people feel safe. Maybe that comes from his Army training. Within a year, the bosses made him the manager of the San Ramos office. Last summer, he asked me to transfer some files to the office's new computer system. When everybody went to lunch, I opened a few and read them. I knew I wasn't supposed to, but the office was empty, and I wasn't going to tell anyone what I found. His customers tell him about their bank accounts, and their medical records, and their driving records because he has to know before he can write a policy.

I know it's private, and I'm not sure how to ask about Nicole, but Dad probably knows why she wasn't in school last fall.

He salts the turkey meatloaf and says, "Each client's information is private."

"Can you tell me what kind of insurance they have?"

"Since when are you interested in insurance, Sandee?"

I stare at my plate.

He leans in and says, "What are you trying to find out?"

"I can't figure out why Nicole Lorca wasn't in *Harvey*."

"Why does it matter? You aren't usually nosy."

I don't know what to say. I barely know Nicole, but almost everybody's guarded around her, like they were with me in the fall. I hate feeling left out. "What's the big secret?"

"Ask her," he says, pushing his chair back from the table. "Do you want to do the dishes or leave them for your mother?"

"I guess we should do them."

"Or we could make her feel useful when she gets home, and you could come and watch basketball with me."

"Bri was your basketball buddy. Not me." The minute I say it, his face changes. I don't mean to hurt him. I never mean to, but I'm not Bri. What about me? Why can't he see me for me? I'm still thinking about Nicole.

He pushes himself back from the table. "Okay, do the dishes for your mom and start your homework. I'll be in the living room if you need me."

I rinse the dishes, while he goes in the other room. I've hurt both my parents today, and I don't know how to make it right.

That night I dream Diego's with Bri instead of Rob. They're digging a hole in our backyard. Diego flings a shovelful of dirt over his shoulder and asks, "Are you sure this is the only way?"

Bri says, "It's too early," and then we're all onstage in the chorus of *Oklahoma!* Diego twirls me around and around, and my skirt swirls. Bri's fiddling so fast his bow flashes in the stage light, and next to him, Rob strums a guitar very slowly.

Then I see a huge flash in the nighttime desert sky. A wall of fire explodes. I cover my eyes, and when I open them, fireworks and flaming ribbons fall through the darkness.

The next thing I know, my alarm is going off. I drag myself to my desk and go back to work on Bowen's assignment, but I can't stop seeing the flames. I sniff. There's no odor of fire or gunpowder anywhere.

CHAPTER TEN

I NEVER SHOP MUCH, unlike Jenn and the other size twos, but being props mistress forces me to. It's fun paying for props from the drama department's petty cash stash. Actors have to buy their own makeup and shoes, but I have a budget, and the drama department pays. This is almost better than a role.

Before rehearsal, I present Ms. G with a bunch of baskets from the Dollar Store, and ask, "Should we ask the girls to decorate them? It might be a way for them to learn more about their characters' likes and dislikes."

"Good idea, Sandee. Tell them after the break. Right now please hold the prompt book and write down any blocking changes today."

My heart pushes in and out against my ribs. "Absolutely, but what happened to Rob?"

"He phoned during lunch and said he had to go home. Just take notes if someone makes a mistake. If someone calls 'Line,' give the next phrase. Don't stop the actors unless they ask for help, okay? I'm the only one who gets to interrupt."

"I'm on it." Once again, I love the sound of that line. I can't stop smiling as I sit next to Ms. G with the prompt book open in front of me, and a sharp pencil in my hand. We aren't even off the first page, though, when Ms. G calls "Cut" and says, "The comedy will be there if you don't try so hard, Diego. Trust the script."

"Okay, boss. How's this?" He takes a deep breath, puffs his chest out, and asks, "Who wants a ol' farm womern anyway?" He's still doing a lifeless John Wayne imitation. Stephanie, who's playing Laurey, sits down on the rehearsal blocks to wait, and Roger, who's playing Curly, sits next to her.

"What do you want, Cord Elam?" Ms. G asks instead of telling him to drop the phony voice. She does that all the time in drama class.

With a goofy grin Diego says, "To get off the stage?"

Nobody looks at him. Two seniors in the chorus snicker. The principals look away, embarrassed. Am I the only one who feels sorry for him?

"I'm asking the character, not the actor, but getting off the stage can be arranged."

Diego's face reddens, and he stuffs his hands in his pockets. "Only kidding, Ms. G."

"What do you want?" she asks again, with more emphasis on *want*.

He scans the stage for help, but everyone who has been in a show knows Ms. G will only accept an answer from him, so they stare at their shoes or the wings. I reach for a couple of stale M&Ms.

"I suppose I'm wrong, but I honestly think I want to make a joke. That's what I was trying to do when you told me to relax."

Ms. G leans forward. "Why do you want to make jokes, Cord Elam?"

"'Cause I cain't git a womern to notice me no other way?" He sounds so much like Cord Elam that I double-check the script. The line's not there. He's improvising—just like he did in my dream.

"Absolutely. If you want the women to notice you, Cord Elam, say it that way. Look at them out of the corner of your eye. Be a shy, lovable bachelor cowboy, joking his way out of an awkward situation."

"Who wants a old farm womern anyway?" He looks down, scuffs at imaginary dirt, and winks at Jenn, who's substituting for Nicole again.

He's good, but did he have to wink at Jenn? Ms. G beams at Diego. "Excellent. Keep going."

Someone taps my shoulder. I look back, and Nicole hands me a folded piece of paper. "Can you give this to Ms. G, please?" I want to open it, but there's a look of fear in her eyes. "It's just a note explaining why I can't stay."

"Again?"

"Please, Sandee, be a friend. I don't have a choice." She stuffs the note into my hand and slips out.

I'm trying to sneak a peek at it when Ms. G stops us again. "What happened to the shy cowboy, Diego?"

"I dunno. I'm not very good at this, Ms. G. Couldn't I just say the lines really fast so we can get on to the songs and stuff?"

"Let's take a few minutes and find out who Cord Elam really is. In fact, this is a good exercise for all of you. Everyone in the theater is going to do this one. Sandee, since you're not a character, we're going to make you the Barbara Walters of the early 1900s."

"What do you mean?"

Ms. G looks excited, the way she does when she's inventing something new for us to try. "Sort of a Nellie Bly. Do you know who she is?"

Jenn waves her hand in the air and says, "She was one of the first female journalists. You'd be good at that, Sandee. You're really good at butting into other people's business."

"Thanks, Jenn." Sarcasm drips from my words.

"Okay, everybody, breathe in character and exhale any negativity you might be carrying around," Ms. G says, looking directly at me. "Breathe in character again, whatever that means to you, and begin walking as your character. How is your character's posture different from yours?" Before anybody can blurt out a response she adds, "Answer in your head." She pauses for a few seconds before she asks, "How does he or she walk? See if you can notice some subtle differences."

The veteran actors know what's coming, and several of us from Beginning Drama remember, but the music kids, like Diego, are puzzled. They go along with it, though, just like I did the first time. If they're like me, they'll keep imagining how their character might respond to things long after the exercise is over.

"Now I want you to start thinking as your character, whatever that means," Ms. G says as we walk around like our characters would. "I'm going to start a sentence, and you're going to let *your character* finish it in your head. No talking, okay? Not even to ask a question. My full name is. . . "

She pauses while I say *Nellie Elizabeth Bly* in my head. Elizabeth sounds like a good middle name to me.

"I live. . . " Ms. G says.

I live in a tiny apartment in New York City with a shop girl named Julie and a waitress named Helen.

"I live with. . . " Ms. G says.

I already named my roommates, so I add, *I live with dreams, hopes, my notebooks, and lots of pencils and pens. I live with a job that makes me wish I had all the rights of a man.*

"Today I want. . . "

. . . to get a really good interview.

"Other people. . . "

. . . aren't as good at interviewing as I am.

"Being scared makes me. . . "

I try to push the word *crazy* out of my head. That's Sandee, not Nellie. I say, *Challenged, challenged, challenged*, trying to stick with Nellie. When I think about being scared, I imagine the call that may come to tell us Bri's fate. Right now, I want to be Nellie. I'll be Sandee again soon enough.

"I have a feeling that a part of me. . . "

. . . is jealous of Bri and— I stop myself. This is Sandee's voice, not Nellie's. Nellie doesn't know Bri. Everyone else is concentrating. *I feel that a part of me . . . has more to offer than she shows the world.* A little thrill runs through me because it's true for Nellie Bly, but it's also true for me. I can play her, and I know it now.

"Once again, I want. . . "

. . . *to find the truth and tell the world.* That works for both of us too. Then Ms. G says, "Cord Elam and Nellie Bly, please stay on stage. Everyone else, come and sit in the audience. Miss Bly, you're going to interview Mr. Elam, an old cowboy from the Oklahoma Territory. Are you ready?"

"Yes, ma'am," I say in a voice that sounds both excited and professional.

I've never called anyone ma'am, but Nellie would.

I drag a table and two chairs out of the wings, sit down, and pull an imaginary notebook and pencil out of my imaginary drawstring purse. Diego's never done an improv except in my dream, so I say, "Mr. Elam, I'm delighted to have this opportunity to talk with you today. Won't you have a seat?"

He grins and walks like he has the same aches and pains as my arthritic grandfather. He takes off an imaginary cowboy hat, lays it on the table, and says, "How can I help you, ma'am?"

"Have you always been a cowhand?"

"Ever since the wife died. If you ain't a landowner, and you don't want to be a storekeeper or a saloonkeeper, it's what you gotta do here in Oklahoma Territory."

The words "Who was your wife and how did she die?" flash through my head. Is that too personal for Nellie Bly? I want us both to stay in character, so I ask, "How do you like working for Aunt Eller?" Most scenes take place on Aunt Eller's ranch. She's an older woman who looks after Laurey, and Laurey is in love with Curly. They're the leads.

"She's a fine womern."

I look into Cord Elam's eyes and not Diego's as I ask, "You don't have a wife anymore, and her husband's gone. Have you ever thought about courting her?" I use my best Nellie Bly voice as I speak.

He shakes his head. Someone laughs, but we both stay in character. "Why not?"

"Are you kidding? She's a grand lady, and I'm an old cowpoke. What would she ever see in me?"

"So you don't think you're as good as Aunt Eller and Laurey?"

"I dunno." Diego's reverting to short answers, so I change the subject.

"What do you do all day?"

"Mend fences. Ride the range. Sometimes tend to sick cattle or strays."

"What's your specialty?"

"Don't have one. Just a lot of experience, ma'am."

"What do you get from your job?"

"A place in the bunkhouse, three meals a day, and a pay envelope at the end of the week."

I had no idea he knew about pay envelopes, and I wonder if he's been doing some research. "What else?" I ask with my imaginary pen poised over my imaginary notebook.

"To be out in the sun on a warm spring day. To hear Miss Eller or Miss Laurey say, 'Thank you, Mr. Elam. That's a job well done.'"

"Scene," Ms. G calls from her director's chair. It doesn't feel like the end of a scene to me, but she says, "You both did an excellent job. Cord Elam, what did you learn about yourself?"

"Do you want him to still be Cord Elam?" I ask before he can say a word.

"I'm sure he heard me say, '*Cord Elam,* what did you learn about yourself?' Miss Bly."

I nod. She wants us both to stay in character. Maybe she's not through with me yet.

Cord Elam says, "I like it when the bosses like my work. I know that Miss Eller and Miss Laurey have the money and the land, but I've got my self-respect. Almost everyone does except Jud. He's kind of a thug."

Everybody laughs, not because Diego's being funny, but because he's exactly right. Jud tries to take Laurey away from Curley in the show, and we hate the character—although the actor's a really nice guy.

Ms. G asks the audience what they believed. They compliment Cord's voice and his walk and his vulnerability. The senior who plays Jud is a big, hulking guy, and he was cast for his size and his amazing voice. He says, "Cord Elam had a real conversation with Nelly Bly. She did good, too. Nobody stole focus and everybody . . . like, had the same goal."

I'm impressed that he noticed Diego's character changes because Jud's good for the part, but he's not much of an actor. He noticed me too, and I'm beaming. Ms. G gave me a chance to act, and I pulled it off.

"Before we take a break, Sandee, do you have an announcement?"

I stare at her

"The baskets?" she asks softly.

"That's right!" Nellie Bly disappears, but I feel empowered without her. "Chorus girls, please take one of the baskets sitting on Ms. G's desk and decorate it as your character would. That way we can tell them apart and find out more about you."

"I want you to start practicing with them, so have them ready in a week, okay?" Ms. G says. "Take a five-minute break. Then we're going to come back and run the act. We might go a little bit over, so text your families and tell them not to wait dinner for you."

The actors open water bottles and check cell phones. Diego glows as one chorus member after another congratulates him.

I feel Nicole's note stuffed in my pocket and hand it to Ms. G, who looks puzzled.

"Nicole didn't want to disturb you."

Ms. G reads it, folds it, and sticks it in her own pocket. "Thanks, Sandee. You did a great job on stage today."

"It was fun," I say and go outside to hang with the cast. Today, I am one of them.

CHAPTER ELEVEN

AT THE END OF rehearsal, I hand Ms. G the prompt book. "Set workday starts at ten tomorrow," she reminds us. "We'll be building some flats, painting, and working on costumes and props, so ask for a job when you arrive unless you already have one. I expect to see all of you promptly at ten."

I barely hear her. Mom and Dad are standing together in the doorway. My heart leaps into my throat. Dad spots me, but he doesn't wave. He pushes his way through the clusters of actors gathering jackets, scripts, and backpacks. "Is Sandee available, Ms. Gittinger?"

"Is everything okay?" I ask at exactly the same moment.

He puts his hand on my shoulder. "Everything's fine. Your mom and I decided that it's been a long time since we've had a family night, so we came by to pick you up."

I can't get a full breath, and I don't know why. This is a good thing. "Where are we going?"

"We'll tell you in the car."

I grab my backpack and am out the door. A second later, I whirl around. "Be right back. I'm supposed to lock up the props," I tell my parents. When I walk back in the theater, Ms. G is covering for me.

"I'm so sorry," I say, but Ms. G holds up a hand to stop me.

"I'm glad you came back, but I completely understand. Forgetting the props is a one-shot deal, okay?"

"Absolutely."

The sun hovers above the ridge, and our shadows are long and narrow as Dad, Mom, and I walk across the empty quad towards the parking lot where our ten-year-old Camry is parked. "Can I drive?" I ask.

"You know it's tough to drive with the sun in your eyes, right?" Dad asks as he hands me his keys.

"I know." I don't tell him that a surge of power rushes through me as I click the button that unlocks the doors.

I slide in behind the steering wheel. Dad sits in the passenger seat, and Mom is relegated to the back. She brushes off the seat and moves Spike's blanket to the floor before she gets in. Spike is Bri's dog, but I'm the one who feeds and walks him these days.

I fasten my seatbelt, check the mirrors, put the key in the ignition, turn it, and ask, "So where are we going?"

"Put 1550 Diablo Road into your GPS," Dad says.

"What city?"

"San Ramos."

"That's like ten minutes from here. That's not much driving practice."

"Would you rather I drive?"

"No."

Mom leans over the console between the seats and says, "Remember to look before you back up."

I back up and shift gears before I say, "Please trust me."

"I do, sweetie. It's just that—"

"Mo-o-om!"

"Susan, she's right. Nothing bad's going to happen, and we're right here."

We drive in silence. I make smooth turns and stay within the speed limit. I finished driver's training before Christmas, and it's already February. If I stay in practice for the next six weeks and two days, I'll pass my driving test on the first try. At least I hope so.

The GPS tells me to turn onto El Cerro, which becomes Diablo, and when we get to 1550, I see a sign for Saint Timothy's Episcopal Church.

"What are we doing here?" Aren't we going out to dinner?

Neither one of them answers, so I pull into a parking space back by the creek. I put the Camry in park, pull up on the emergency brake, turn off the engine, and ask again.

"Your mother has something to say to you."

I reach into my jacket pocket for my M&Ms, but I slide my hand back out without taking any. "Mom?"

"You remember when I went to the Blue Star Moms meeting a few days ago?"

"Sure." I see the dark circles under her eyes in my rearview mirror.

"They told me about a support group that meets here."

"Support group?"

"Support for families of people serving in the war. The Blue Star Moms run it."

"Am I going to be the only teenager there?" My throat tightens as I speak.

"No. It's for families. Didn't I just say that?" She reaches into her purse, takes out a lipstick, and adds a new layer.

"You look fine, Susan," Dad says, and at the same time I ask, "Are we going to talk about Bri in front of a bunch of strangers?"

"No. We're going to listen to other people's stories. If they ask who you are, say, 'I'm Sandee and my brother's been missing in Afghanistan for almost eight months.'"

"Ready, kiddo?" Dad asks as he opens his car door. Of course I'm ready. Willing is another matter.

The woman who greets us at the door is Mom's age. She has red hair and wears more lipstick and eyeliner than she needs. She looks like she's trying to hide her real identity. Her muffin top bulges under her tan sweater. I pull my coat tightly around me.

"We're the Masons," Mom says in her professional voice. She

sounds more normal than she has in months. If the Blue Star Moms can do this for her, I hope she'll be a regular at their meetings.

The greeter smiles, shakes Mom's hand, then Dad's, and says, "Please get a cup of coffee or a bottle of water and find a seat. We'll start in just a minute." Then she turns to the family behind us.

A young women holding a baby stands on the far side of the room, chatting with a woman who could be either her mom or her mother-in-law. They're both drinking coffee in Styrofoam cups. They look weary. I know the feeling.

A short woman wearing a red silk blouse and a navy pencil skirt rings a gong and says, "My name's Judy, and I'm your chairperson. My daughter has a traumatic brain injury, and she has been at the Veteran's Hospital in Martinez for the last nine weeks." People sit down, scoop babies into their laps, and a large woman with a long braid hanging down her back takes half a dozen rowdy toddlers to another room.

I turn to Dad and whisper, "What's a traumatic brain injury?"

He can't look at me as he says, "Bruising or bleeding in the brain. It happens after a violent impact. Bob Woodruff has one."

"The reporter on ABC?" Dad made me watch enough war news that I remember seeing the dark-haired man doing human-interest stories about soldiers in hospitals. He turns the injured side of his face away from the camera as much as he can. Even though he doesn't quite look normal, he sounds recovered to me.

Everyone's staring, and I realize it's my turn to speak. "Sorry," I say. "I'm Sandee, and my brother disappeared in Afghanistan almost eight months ago." My face feels like it's on fire. Everyone's staring, but it's not at all like when I played Nellie Bly this afternoon. That was a role; this is real. Everybody says, "Hi, Sandee," and I feel like an extra in a movie about AA.

Judy turns the meeting over to the speaker. His name is Tom. His son, a sergeant on his second tour of duty, has been missing for twenty-one months. "He signed up after five colleges rejected him. I encouraged him to join the Army and learn a trade," Tom says, but his voice breaks. I can't look at him. I stare at the table with the coffee pot and Styrofoam cups instead, and I blink back tears. For some reason the guy playing Jud pops into my head. He probably won't get into college either, unless it's music school. If he goes into the Army. . .

I shudder. *Focus, focus, focus.* That mantra stops the scary thoughts sometimes.

When Tom's done, a blonde woman with big arms and thighs tells about her son, who disappeared four years ago. "People tell me to move on, but how can I do that?" she asks. My throat swells.

Dad stares at his hands while she speaks. He takes short breaths and bites his lip. I hope he won't talk. Mom sits on the far side of him and dabs at her eyes with a used Kleenex.

Then a woman with bird legs and skinny braids all over her head tells us her husband was deployed six weeks ago. "He ran our house like a military barracks, and I thought we'd have peace once he was gone, but the silence is awful." I know what she means. Bri always overshadowed me, but he's larger than life now that he's not here.

When it's time for a break, the woman who greeted us at the door goes from group to group offering cupcakes. Mom shakes her head. I excuse myself, head for the bathroom, and on the way, I stuff a handful of M&Ms into my mouth.

"Do they help?" a girl with a husky voice asks. She's taller and slimmer than me, and she wears a yellow pullover and gray chinos that hug her hips. Her blue-black hair hangs straight, almost to her waist. She tucks it behind her ears while she waits for me to answer.

"You'll never know unless you try." I hold out the package, and she shakes her head slowly. "I'll bet you're afraid of what chocolate would do to that trim body."

"Are you using them to feel better?"

"Excuse me?"

She grins and says, "You heard me. Are you hungry or are you eating those because you miss somebody?"

OMG. She doesn't even know me. "Can you always read people so well?"

"I recognize coping mechanisms, and yours is a lot less harmful than some. I'm Tessa Kwan."

"Sandee Mason."

"My sister, Kayla, went to Afghanistan nineteen months ago."

"That's where my brother disappeared. His patrol went out, and they never came back."

"That's terrible," she says. Nothing more.

"What happened to Kayla?"

"War messed with her head. Literally. She came back in a coma, but the doctors say she could open her eyes and speak anytime."

Wow. She's so calm. How does she do that? "Do you think she could have known my brother?"

"Anything's possible."

I stare at my shoes. What am I supposed to say? Whatever it is, the words won't come.

"Tell you what. Call me if you want to talk." She hands me a card that says Blue Star Moms. "The card is theirs, but the phone number on the back is mine."

I turn it over. She has written her name and a phone number.

"There aren't too many sibs around here, and sometimes it helps to talk. Call me right now, and put me in your cell, okay?"

When her phone rings, she says, "Hello? Hello?" as if I'm not standing next to her. We both laugh. The adults around us turn and stare, and that makes us laugh harder.

I save her contact info, and she says, "Why don't you sit with me instead of your parents?"

Sitting next to her makes it easier to listen, and since we are across the room from my parents, I can keep an eye on them without their noticing.

That night I dream that Bri is nine again. He's with Rob and a bunch of other guys at the park where they all played baseball, and all the guys keep chanting, "Shrimp-o. Shrimp-o" until Bri says, "Knock it off. She's only a kid."

Then fireworks stream through the desert sky, but this time blackness follows instead of flames.

My palms are furry. I open my eyes, and look at my hand. It's clutching Spike's fur. Spike adopted me after Bri left home. Now he nuzzles his nose under my hand.

Sometimes I have dreams that come true in some unexpected way, like the one about Diego and the improv. He's not in drama class, but we still did an improv together. Once, I dreamed about a rejection letter three days before a computer camp wrote to tell me they were full. They said to try again next year, but I dreamed about it right before I heard from them, as if my brain knew before the letter came. No wonder a dream about fireworks in the desert terrifies me.

If only Bri would say, "It's going to be all right." I listen, but I hear nothing other than my dad's snoring in the next room.

CHAPTER TWELVE

THE NEXT MORNING, DIEGO and I skirt the puddles on our way to set workday. Diego wears jeans with holes in the knees and a shirt with paint stains that I've never seen before. He carries a sack with plastic garlic and peppers and a stack of tablecloths that his mother loaned us. It's part of the picnic stuff on the props list. I'm grateful everyone's helping, but my head is still full of the Blue Moms support group and my dream of the desert. I can't talk about either one.

Instead, I concentrate on the noise my paint-dappled cords make as my thighs rub together. Then I think about the props shifting around in my backpack. I carry the Little Wonder, which is supposed to have dirty pictures inside, an old glass bottle that Mom said would pass for smelling salts, an eggbeater, a ladle, a tablecloth, and the triangle and ringer that her boss, Alicia, said we could borrow from Generation to Generation. I put my thumbs under the straps of my backpack because it's banging against my jacket.

I'm still shifting its weight when Diego says, "So if you decided to cancel last night, why didn't you call me? We were going to the movies together, remember?"

I put my hand on the sleeve of his jacket. "I'm sorry, Diego. I didn't even think about it."

He keeps his eyes straight ahead. "Then you won't mind that Jenn and I went to the party at Rob's, will you?"

Low blow! "You can go to a party with anybody you want." I sound snooty, and I don't care. He knows how I feel about Jenn.

"You're the one who bailed. You couldn't even text from the car?"

"Dad let me drive."

"Fine."

"We went . . . we went . . . You heard my dad. We did something as a family. No big deal."

"Fine," he says again.

He doesn't deserve this, but I can't get the right words out. Last night unsettled me. I can't explain it. Not yet. I have no reason to feel embarrassed, but I do. After workday, I'll call Tessa. Maybe she can explain why I feel so weird and shy. Diego and I don't say another word for the rest of the trip, and it isn't a comfortable silence.

The din of power saws and hammers inside the rehearsal room drowns out every thought in my head. We take our props to Ms. G, who stands behind her desk, studying a blueprint. She looks at our collection and says, "Good job." She pulls her keys out of the pocket of her jeans, gives them to me, and says, "Lock up the props and return the keys to my hand. Don't leave them on the desk." Then she goes back to the blueprint.

I'm about to return her keys when I spot a girl who looks just like Tessa. She's surrounded by sawdust, wearing a T-shirt with a City of San Ramos logo, and she's holding a tape measure for Rob.

"I have my own work to do, Rob. I have to paint the porch decorations," she says as she finger-combs the sawdust out of her long, black ponytail.

"That's why you don't get better jobs, Tessa. You're not a team player."

"Excuse me?"

"You don't understand that we're an ensemble."

"You've got to be—" She sees me coming across the room and stops herself. "Sandee, right? You're working on the show?"

"She's my assistant, Tessa. If you're going to be a part of this, you should learn who's who." Rob tugs on his paint-speckled T-shirt.

"I'm impressed, Sandee. You any good with a paint brush?" She ignores Rob, who stands over the flat, snapping his tape measure.

"Not really. I'm much better at taking photos than painting pictures."

"Well, I could use some help if you'd like to give it a try. I'll show you what you need to do." Both Tessa and Rob stare at me like I'm a prize in some contest I don't remember entering.

"Sure, but I need to talk to Rob about the surrey first."

"Go ahead, but don't let him call all the shots, okay?" she whispers as she walks past me.

Rob holds out the tape measure Tessa thrust at him. "Come here, Sandee. You can hold one end of the tape measure while we talk."

I stare at Tessa and wonder why I didn't find out about this last night.

"Sandee, do I need to get someone else to handle the tape measure?"

I shake my head.

"We can't afford to make any mistakes."

I stoop down, hook the end of the tape measure over the end of the board and ask, "Any ideas where we can get an old wagon to use for the surrey base?"

He punches the dimensions into the calculator on his cell. "How would you find one? How would you get it here?"

"Well, um, I haven't figured that part out yet, but if you know someone with a truck, we'd have a way to get it here. Do you?"

"Who laid this stupid thing out?" he asks. I have no idea, of course. He rubs his forefingers against both temples. "Sandee, I really can't answer your silly questions right now. Go help Tessa paint the set decorations, okay?"

"The surrey's just as important as the flats," I say as I walk away, "but I can handle it." If only that were the truth.

I make my way around drying flats and costume girls stitching up vests to get to Tessa, who's outlining the window frames we're going to paint on the front of Aunt Eller's house.

"Can you paint between these lines?" she asks.

"Sure. I guess." The truth is I don't really know. I used to draw outside the lines in my coloring books.

"Start here." I love being trusted. "Tape the edges to hide any splatters, and fill in the space between them."

"The tape will cover my mistakes, right?"

"Exactly." She doesn't take her eyes off the window.

"So, what colors are we using?" I ask once she finishes the line along the window's edge.

"Use the lighter one here and the darker one on Jud's shack. He's the villain, right?"

I nod. "You and Ms. G are the only ones making sense this morning. Diego and Rob are both acting weird," I say as I start stretching blue painter's tape next to the pencil lines she's drawn on the flats.

"They're probably overcompensating."

"For what?"

"They're hungover."

She has to be wrong. Diego doesn't drink.

"The drama kids are notorious for their Friday night parties at Rob's. He has one almost every week." She pries the lid off the eggshell paint before she sees my face. I must look as confused as I feel because she says, "Nobody's told you about Rob's parties?"

"I went to one the Friday before the cast list was posted, but we just hung out and watched a DVD of the original *Dracula*."

"Everybody had a beer in their hands, right?" How does she know? How did I forget so quickly? "Last year there was way too much drinking and using at Rob's parties. That's why Ms. G wrote those contracts everybody signed. The administration said she had to put a stop to it or they were going to notify the police." She hands me a small, flat brush and says, "Put a coat of eggshell on the window sashes, okay?" She points to the spaces where the wood runs between the panes in an old-fashioned, four-paned window and says, "When it's dry, we'll come back and add some texture and depth."

I nod. My head is still back at Rob's party. Diego and Jenn went to another one last night. I don't want to go back because Rob kept giving me beer during *Dracula*. He invited me again, but I told him I had a family commitment, and this week, that line became true.

I dip the flat brush into the eggshell and carefully paint between the tapelines that mark the sashes. The paint rolls off the brush and onto the flat smoothly and easily. Once I get into a painting rhythm, Tessa asks, "So, was the support group what you thought it would be?"

"It was okay."

"Just okay?" I paint faster. She waits.

The silence gets bigger between us until I say, "How can you stand having your sister in a coma?" My face grows warm, and I hope she isn't looking at me.

"What choice do I have? Kayla wants me to be happy."

"I hate everybody thinking of Brian whenever they see me, but I miss him. I'd love to know where he is and how he is."

"Be careful what you wish for."

My stomach and chest tighten until I'm afraid I'll throw up. "Does the awkwardness ever go away?"

"You mean the way people look at you when they pass you in the hall?" I nod because my throat's swelling again. "And the people who can't make eye contact when they talk to you, or the ones who won't speak because they don't know what to say?"

I glance over. She's challenging me, just like she did last night when she saw me consuming the M&Ms. She catches my look and says, "You can't avoid your feelings, Sandee. You have to face them. Isn't that why your parents brought you last night?"

"Sure, but they need to face their own feelings too." I repaint the same spot over and over. I shouldn't have said that. It sounds terrible, but it's the truth.

"When your brother's been away as long as my sister, you'll know that there are no 'wrong' feelings. Everything's valid."

We continue painting in silence. Eventually I say, "Are you in the same class as Nicole?"

"She's a junior and I'm a senior, but she's in Advanced Art with me. I could use her painting skills, but she's not here."

I look around and realize she's right. Nicole's missing, even though Ms. G said everyone had to be here. Behind us, Rob's telling Diego how and where to hold the tape measure.

"Change of subject," I say. "Any ideas where we can get a working surrey?"

"Could you build it on a flatbed trailer like they use for the homecoming floats?" she asks as she textures a barrel for Aunt Eller's porch.

"We need the big, wooden wheels with spokes instead of tires. This really should be set construction's job—not mine."

"It sounds more like a set piece than a prop to me, but we'll probably all have to work together on it." She picks up a clean sponge, dabs it in a chocolate brown, and changes the subject. "Do you know how casts and armies are alike?"

"What are you talking about?"

"They're both ensembles. Everybody marches in step towards the same goal, right?"

"You're right, but an Army is—"

"Think about it. The general's the director. The majors are the principals, the captains are the crew heads, the privates are the chorus and crew, but none of us can do our job alone, and we all have a common purpose."

"When Bri disappeared, he stopped being an anonymous chorus member and became a . . . I don't know, a supporting player?"

"Exactly. At least, he's a supporting player to those who are looking for him."

"That's grim. He shouldn't have to go missing to matter. Do you ever dream about Kayla?"

"All the time."

"I dream about Bri, and sometimes I hear his voice. Does that sound crazy?"

"No. You're stressed, and if the daydreams seem real, then you believe you're hearing his voice."

"I suppose," I say, even though I'm sure his voice is more real than a daydream.

CHAPTER THIRTEEN

WHILE THE WINDOWS DRY, Tessa shows me how to weather the columns on Aunt Eller's porch. I'm glad to avoid Rob. I'd rather talk to Tessa. I rock back on my heels and watch her work before I ask, "When you got the news about Kayla, how did your best friends react?"

"My best friend understood . . . maybe because we'd been going out for nearly a year." She kneels to get to the bottom of the water barrel on the side of the porch.

"So your best friend is your boyfriend?"

"Was. He went to the Art Academy in September, and we don't see each other as much, but he still texts."

"Does he have a new girlfriend?"

"Not as far as I know. He's getting ready for an art show they're doing at his school, and that takes all his time."

"I love that he's your best friend even if you're not going out anymore."

"What about you?" She twists around to face me. "Do you have a boyfriend? "

"Not since we split up in the seventh grade."

"Aren't you and Diego a couple? He walks you home often enough."

Am I this obvious? "No-o-o-o-o. We walk each other home," I protest.

Tessa stares at me like she did last night when she caught me stuffing my face with M&Ms. There's no way to fake it with her.

"OMG. Diego was your seventh-grade boyfriend, wasn't he?" Her eyes dance. "I can see it in your face. Do you want to get back together?" I squeeze the sponge way too tight, splatter paint all over my hand and the floor, and reach for a rag. "Well?" she asks as I clean up.

"I didn't think I cared until he started flirting with someone in the cast. She won't give him the time of day, though."

"Jenn?" I keep mopping up the paint splatter. My face gets hot. "Don't look so shocked. I looked across the room when she walked in, and I saw her hand Diego a Starbucks cup."

I start tapping the sponge against another column before I say, "We walk together because he's my neighbor, and now he's in the show, even though he didn't try out."

"That sucks." I keep painting. "Actually, maybe it doesn't," she continues. "This way you get to see him every day."

I stare at the aged post on Aunt Eller's porch and think about the way Diego and I watched movies with a bowl of popcorn sitting between us over winter break. We talk about the way things used to be in seventh grade, when we were crushing on each other and Bri and Rob were hanging out in the basement or Bri's room.

"Diego didn't get awkward when Bri went missing. He hung out and listened and sat with me while I cried. Weeks went by, and he said Bri would want me to get on with my life. It's hard not to be friends with someone like that."

Suddenly Rob's screams drown out the hammering, the handsaw, and all the conversations. "Are you bleeding?" I scream across the rehearsal room.

Everybody stops. Everyone turns. It's like we're all choreographed in a scene that stars Rob.

"What is the matter with everybody today?" he screams, waving a hammer in the air. "The long boards go on the outside, and the short boards stay on the inside. What's wrong with you? You've built flats for your mom's shows, Jenn."

"It was a mistake," Jenn says. I've never seen her skin so pasty.

Diego gets in Rob's face. "You can't talk to her that way." *Way to defend her, Diego.* It's not that I want him defending Jenn. It's that I love seeing him put Rob in his place. "If you don't stop yelling, I'm walking out, and if I go, I'm taking Jenn with me. You don't get to abuse us just because you're having a bad day."

I can't stop smiling in spite of the fact that he's defending Jenn. Too bad she doesn't appreciate it. "Whatever happened to being an ensemble?" she asks everyone with those doe-eyes she gets whenever she needs approval.

Rob gives her the same look Bowen gives me in math class. "You're of no benefit to the ensemble if you can't build a simple flat."

"No value? Last night you said I. . . " She stares at the sawdust on the floor and sniffs.

Rob speaks slowly with the practiced patience of Ms. Harris, who teaches the developmentally delayed. "Take off the cornerstones, Jenn. Realign the boards. Then nail new cornerstones on. Diego, help her or make yourself useful elsewhere. I can't spend all day on this one flat."

"You suck as a leader," Diego says loud enough for everyone to hear, including Ms. G.

Rob sputters, but no words come out. He whirls around and storms out of the rehearsal room. One of leads gives Diego a thumbs-up. She's holding up her cell phone. I'll bet she taped Rob's whole meltdown.

"What a loser," one of the leads says, and a bunch of them gather around the cell phone chanting, "Loser, loser, loser."

The girl with the phone makes a slashing gesture under her throat. As soon as they're quiet she tells us, "If you missed Rob's explosion, check YouTube for reruns."

Poor Rob. Diego's right. He sucks at being a leader, but even Rob doesn't deserve to be recorded while he's having a meltdown.

Tessa leans over and whispers, "Diego's really something."

"I've never seen him like that. Maybe he's growing up."

"Maybe he's waiting for you to make a move. Jenn doesn't appreciate him. Do you?" Her voice is casual, but her question is so unexpected that I freeze. I scan the theater. Diego and Jenn stretch muslin over the last frame. A boy I haven't met checks the lamps in the stage lights overhead, plugging them in one after another. Almost everyone else has gone home. A few minutes later, Rob returns and corners Ms. G behind her desk.

She sees me staring at the two of them, beckons, and Tessa takes the sponge from me and says, "Go."

"What's up?" I ask Ms. G as I rub my paint-stained hands on some paper towels lying on the floor near her desk.

"Can you make a list of the props we still need? We'll ask the cast to help with whatever you can't get."

This is not what I expected, but I say, "We need a base for the surrey, and the top, and we need something we can use for the guns and rifles."

"A starter pistol or two might work," she says.

Rob, who's still standing beside her, says, "They won't look real." I roll my eyes, but I keep my mouth shut. Let him hang himself. "I know we can come up with something better," he says when we all ignore him.

"I'm not sure where we can get something that's both real and disabled. Sandee, does your family know any gun collectors?" Ms. G asks.

I like the way she avoids asking Rob. Too bad guns scare me so much right now. *What would Bri do?* A minute later, I say, "What about the rifle clubs?"

She shakes her head. "They preserve guns. They won't disable them."

"Military families?" I ask, even though I know my father doesn't keep any guns in our house.

"Tessa comes from a military family and so do you. Why don't you see what the two of you can come up with?"

"What about the surrey?" I ask again.

"Call other high schools that have done the show, and see if you can get any leads."

"Do you think we can find something on one of the ranches up on Pine Mountain?" We had a class picnic up there in eighth grade, and I think of it at the oddest moments. "Maybe someone up there has an old wagon we could use."

"Why don't you Google high school productions of *Oklahoma!* and contact the drama teachers in those schools before you start calling ranches?" Ms. G asks.

"Good plan."

"Who's going to call Nicole, Sam, Keith, and Mary about their absences if Sandee doesn't do it?" Rob asks.

"You are, Rob. Maybe listening to somebody else's problems is exactly what you need. Besides, I don't want you calling other drama departments on behalf of us right now."

"I told you I was sorry."

"Yes, you did, and once you call the people who were absent today, we'll say no more about it."

"He's busted," Diego whispers.

"Shut up, Diego." The muscles in Rob's neck tighten, and I know he isn't really sorry at all. He grabs a broom, while Ms. G goes over to talk to one of the costumers.

Diego leans in and whispers, "When he came back, she told him we're a school, and he said, 'What about making the shows as professional as possible?' Then, she said, 'A leader knows how to do that without demeaning his workers. I thought you had your temper under control, Rob. I don't want to see any more of it.'"

"Ooo. Fireworks!"

"Very quiet fireworks." I grin. Diego nods and winks at me. "Watch the rerun on YouTube tonight."

CHAPTER FOURTEEN

I EXPECT TO WALK home with Diego after we put all the tools away, but Dad's waiting outside the rehearsal room.

"Ready to go, kiddo?"

"Why are you here?"

"Why do you ask so many questions?" He puts his arm around my shoulder. "It turned into a beautiful day, so I thought you might like a ride."

Why would I want a ride on a beautiful day? The walnuts at the edge of the campus are blooming against a pure-blue sky. The previous night's storm carried away the smog, and the air sparkles. Green grass grows early in California, and it's sprouting on the hills behind the creek on the far side of San Ramos Boulevard.

"Can I drive?" He doesn't hear me. "If I can't drive, can we at least take Diego? It's not like it's out of our way," I say in a louder voice.

"Sure. Get in back, son."

While Dad puts the car in gear, I turn to Diego and ask, "What did you think of workday?"

"It was okay," he mutters, rubbing his temples the way Rob did earlier.

"You like working with Jenn all day?"

"Jenn's cool."

"She looked kind of sick to me. I hope nothing's going around. It would be horrible for the show."

"Chill, Sandee. Nothing's going around. It's Saturday and some of us are tired." He sticks his earbuds in, and when I ask what he's listening to, he ignores me.

Five minutes later, I wave my hand in his face and say, "Feel better," as Dad pulls up to the curb. Diego waves, but his sparkling smile isn't there. "If he's got the flu, it had better be the twenty-four-hour kind. He can't afford to miss rehearsal," I tell Dad.

"You're really into this show, aren't you?" he says more to the windshield than to me.

"Yeah! Ms. G loves the props I've collected, and you know that girl I met last night? Tessa?" He doesn't answer. "She was there too. We talked about all kinds of things. Do you think Diego might be interested in me again?"

Dad stares at the steering wheel. I open my door, but he stops me. "Honey, there's something I have to tell you—something that your mom and I have to tell you."

"You're not separating, are you?"

They talked about it last fall. There'd been this awful silence after Bri went missing—except when I was in my room with the door closed, doing homework, or listening to music, or trying to sleep. Then I'd hear them fighting. Mom would scream, "I can't stand doing nothing."

"You think I like this?" Dad would ask.

"We need to hire someone to go over there and look for him."

"You read too many spy novels, Susan. If the Army can't find him, there's nothing we can do. Trust me. I know the Army."

One night I heard her say, "He's our son, and if you don't care about him, we should separate." The pain in her voice brought tears to my eyes.

So now, when I hear him say, "No, it's nothing like that. We're not separating," I breathe a sigh of relief. It goes away a second later when he says, "We got some news today."

My stomach flutters the way it does before Bowen passes back a math test or Ms. G announces a new show. "I'm afraid it isn't good news." I stare at my hands. There's a lump in my throat. "It's about your brother." My stomach flips. I know what he's going to say. I'm afraid I might throw up. He reaches over and puts a hand on my arm. "They found his body."

I can't think. Then a million thoughts charge through my brain at once. I hear myself say, "Whose car is parked in the driveway?"

What I want to say is how could this happen, but I know the answer. Dad once told both Bri and me that sometimes serving your country means losing your life.

"It belongs to Judy, the woman who ran the meeting last night. She gave all the new people her number, and I called her before I came to pick you up."

"She doesn't know us."

Dad takes his hand off my arm and hugs me. "When we got the news, your mom couldn't talk. She started rocking back and forth, and I knew she needed someone other than a retired Army captain to talk to, so I gave the woman a call. I've lost people in combat before, but your mom has never lost a son. She's in shock. So I need you to be strong for her. Can you do that?"

I stare at the house that Bri will never see again. It hasn't changed, but it will never be the same again either.

"So they'll ship him back in a box?" I whisper.

"In a coffin. They'll ship as much as they can find of him in a coffin." His eyes are moist, and he can't look at me.

"As much as they can find?"

"Apparently some body parts were . . . missing," he says to the steering wheel.

"Why were some . . . ?" I can't finish my sentence.

"Sometimes torture precedes murder. Sometimes bodies are blown to bits. He was a tough man. My son was a man. He was proud to go." A tear trickles down his face.

Why aren't I crying? Isn't that what you do when someone dies? There are no tears, though—just a wall of acid wetness in my stomach lining and a weight hanging from my heart. This can't be real. Maybe I'm dreaming again. "Okay, Dad. Now you say, 'Wake up, Sandee. Dream's over.'"

"It's not a dream, honey. You can feel my hand on your arm, right?" I stare at it; I can't speak. "Just nod." I nod. "I wish it were a dream. I wish you could wake up and come to me because Bri and Rob called you a baby. I'm sorry, but this is real, and we have to face it."

"Bri promised he'd come back." The words squeak out. He's my big brother. We fight, and I tell him I hate him, and he and Rob tease me, but we do it because we know there's always tomorrow and next week and next year.

If it's a good day, a big brother helps you with your science project. If it's a bad day, he tells you you're a pest, but that night he lets you practice your speech for English without judging it the way Mom or Dad would. Sometimes a brother teaches you how to make a bully back down—or tells you high school will be great, and you'll be just fine there.

"Does Emma know?" I ask Dad. Emma is Bri's girl. Was. How am I going to get used to this? Emma's a freshman at UC Berkeley. The day he left, Bri told Mom and Dad, "I'm counting on you to take care of her as if she were your daughter because she will be when I get back." Then he put a hand on my shoulder and said, "I'm counting on you to leave your mark on San Ramos High. Make the world a little better and have some fun while you're at it." He was so solemn and serious that he didn't sound like himself. Maybe it was the Army talking.

Dad says, "I asked Emma to call us. I'm afraid she'll suspect the worst when she gets the message, but there's never an easy way to say this kind of thing."

"So what do I do?"

"Go in and hug your mom. Tell her you love her. We'll take this one step at a time."

I'll hug my mom, but how can we handle uncharted territory like this one step at a time when we don't even know what direction we're supposed to go in?

CHAPTER FIFTEEN

"I'M SO SORRY, MOM," I say the minute I see her huddled into a corner of our floral-print sofa, clutching a gold pillow. It looks ridiculously cheerful against her curled body. She clutches a wad of crumpled Kleenex and stares at a collection of unlit candles in the middle of the two-tiered coffee table, but I don't think she sees them. Judy sits in the armchair next to the sofa. She's dressed in dark jeans and a loose black turtleneck today.

"Mom?"

She says nothing. "Can she hear me?" I ask Judy.

"I think so. She's in shock. Come sit next to her and give her a hug." When I do, Mom doesn't respond. I'm not her firstborn, but I'm still here.

That's a horrible thought, and I push it away as Judy says, "You're the younger sister, right?"

"I'm Sandee." I can't take my eyes off my mom. I can't stop her tears or my own. "Mom, it's me. Sandee. I'm here. Dad's here. I'm so sorry about Bri."

She puts one arm around me. I know she's heard. I don't understand why she can't speak.

Dad helps her to her feet. "Come on, Susan. We're going to the kitchen to get you some fresh tea."

"Sandee, I know your mom loves you very much," Judy says as

soon as Mom and Dad are out of the room. "She's in shock. That's why she can't respond."

I know, but seeing Mom that way scares me. "You ran the meeting last night." I don't know what else to say.

She smiles. "That's exactly right. You have more presence of mind than many young women your age. Do you know that?"

I love being called a young woman, even in the midst of this awful moment. "I guess so." I feel guilty not talking about Bri.

"Your mom can't speak right now because she's in shock, but you and your dad will be better for her than any doctor."

Why does she have to say Mom's in shock again? Does she think I'm in shock too? "Are you a doctor?" I ask because I don't know what else to say.

She takes a deep breath and sips her tea. "I'm a psychologist. I run the support meetings because my daughter has a TBI. Do you know what that is?"

"Kind of."

I looked at her again. Her broad cheekbones look familiar. "Is your daughter named Kayla?"

"How did you know?"

"You're Tessa's mom?"

"Yes, I am," she says with a proud smile that she can't contain, even when she's on a condolence call. "Now, while your dad's taking care of your mom, I'd like to know what's happening with you."

The shock about Bri tingles just under my skin. "It seemed like we were waiting forever to hear about him. Now I want to go back to waiting."

She nods.

"I can't believe he's gone." What is there to say? Everything is trivial crap. "He doesn't even know that his buddy Rob and I are working on *Oklahoma!* together or that I'm struggling in math or that I'm going to get my driver's license in a few more weeks. Well, maybe he knows about the math. I always struggle in math."

Why am I babbling like this? I wonder as Judy says, "What do you wish you could say to him?" She cocks her head as if she cares.

I want to say, "What difference will it make?"—to her, not Bri—but that would only embarrass me. Bri too. After a minute, I curl my legs under me and whisper, "I miss you, Bri." An official Army photo of him stares at us from the wall. It hangs right next to Dad's photo from the first Iraq war. I stare at it and ignore Judy. "You're in my dreams, Bri. I thought that meant you were alive. How could I have been so dumb?"

"Nothing is dumb, I promise you," Judy says. She reaches over and puts her hand on my forearm just like Dad did in the car. "Anything else?"

I pull out of her reach. "I don't know." Tears well up in my eyes as I say it. Stubbornly, I blink them away. "Do you work for the Army or something?"

"The chaplain calls me when he needs a volunteer to help with a family's grief. You know it was your dad who called me, and not the Army, don't you?" I nod, still blinking back tears. "You can say anything to me."

"Would it be okay if I went into Bri's room?" Why do I want to do that? Is it even still Bri's room if he's dead? The word *dead* thunks around inside my head like a steel ball, and I shudder.

"I don't see why not. Do you want me to come with you?"

I shake my head and go up the stairs, avoiding the familiar creak on the third step from the bottom. Bri and I used to pretend the house was haunted whenever it creaked, but that would be so wrong now.

Mom cleans Bri's room every week, always taking time to polish the track trophies on his bookshelves. He has an A's Pennant on the wall and a dartboard on his closet door. I take one of the darts out, finger it, then cross the room, and throw it.

It lands in the wall.

Carefully I pull it out and rub a couple paint flakes over the pinhole. Then I return it to the exact place where Bri last threw it. I hold my hand there, but I can't feel his energy. Ms. Schroeder, who teaches Environmental Science, told us energy lingers. If it does, I can't feel it.

I go to his window, lift the shade, and look out on the back lawn. Bri's too real to be gone. If death stole him away, it can take me too.

I place my hand against the dartboard, lightly at first, and then with all my might. No matter how hard I push, I feel the dart-pierced surface and nothing more.

I sit at Bri's desk. A graduation picture of him with an arm around his girlfriend, Emma, is pinned on the bulletin board right next to his Student Council Certificate of Appreciation. Did she feel a chill when he died or see him at the end of her bed at night? I read a story where that happened, but it has never happened to me. Did I dream about him on the night he died—or feel something as he left earth—or even see fireworks in the desert sky? What am I supposed to do with all the things I still have to say to him?

A couple of times after we learned he disappeared eight months ago, I Googled "psychic + Berkeley." Maybe that sounds silly, but some of them are so confident when they channel people on TV shows. Surely the whole audience can't be trying to trick us. Every Google ad said I needed a credit card, and I wasn't about to ask Mom or Dad if I could borrow a credit card to call a psychic.

I'm pretty sure there's a connection between this world and the next one. A girl in my English class says she has seen angels. I want Bri to be my guardian angel if he's on the other side. Every time I hear his voice, I ask him to show me what to do, but whenever I ask, he shuts up. It's like he picks the times when I get to hear from him—just like any older brother.

I stare at the photos on his bulletin board. I want to take them down and put them in my room, but Mom and Dad and Emma have first dibs. Rob too.

Tears fill my eyes. Can a psychic show me where Bri is now and how he got there? Can anybody? I touch the graduation photo again and hear the hinges of his door squeak. "Bri?"

The door creaks. I whirl around in his desk chair. Rob peeks through. "Can I come in?"

"What are you doing here?" I ask, sitting up straighter.

"I came as soon as I read about it on Facebook. He's gone, isn't he?"

A wet, acidic feeling runs down the walls of my stomach again. "What are you talking about?" I ask even though I know.

Rob stands just inside the door, as if he's afraid. "Jenn posted that an Army car came to your house. A chaplain got out. She said that Bri was probably gone and you needed your space."

"You're kidding, right?" I ask, even though he's clearly not. I close my eyes and bite my lip, hoping that pain will stop the much bigger one in my heart.

Rob wraps his arms around me. My breath comes shorter and shorter.

He's holding me up. I wriggle away and lean against the wall.

"I'm so sorry. I don't know what to say. You want me to call her?" Rob asks.

I can't get a grip on this. I don't even know what the Army told my parents, and Jenn has already broadcast it on Facebook?

I stare out the window at the tree house where Diego and I used to sit and spy on Rob and Bri. A new crop of buds pokes out from the branches. Life goes on, whether Bri's here or not. Did a bomb or an IED take him out—or a suicide bomber?

Maybe Jenn knows. Apparently she's the authority on all things Brian. I sit on Bri's bed and hug my knees to my chest. I will stay strong. Bri would want it that way.

"Would you put it on Facebook without talking to me?" I hate the quiver in my voice.

"No," Rob says. "She said we should leave you alone, but I came anyway. She thought if she told people, you wouldn't have to."

"How stupid."

"You're not the only one who misses him, you know. He and I both had the same enemies, the jocks and the loudmouths. When my dad left, hanging out with Bri made me less alone. I was almost like a member of your family."

"I'm glad you ignored Jenn." I smile at him for the first time since his meltdown at workday. Poor guy.

"I came because I thought Bri would want me to."

"Why?"

"He sent me an e-mail from Basic Training and told me to watch out for you. I wrote back and reminded him that he was the big brother, but I'd try. I came over to see how you were doing. Is that strange?"

"No stranger than anything else happening today." I stare into our backyard. Bri won't be at any more barbecues.

After a minute Rob says, "Do you want me to leave you alone?" I shrug. "Why don't you call me when you want to talk?"

I hear the door close behind him. I stare into the yard, and see Spike, lying next to his doghouse with his nose between his paws. Poor boy. He has no idea that Bri is never coming back.

CHAPTER SIXTEEN

THE NEXT MORNING, I sit at our kitchen table, drinking herbal tea and texting Diego. Dad sticks his head through the kitchen door and says, "We need to talk."

I text, "Dad's here. Later" and hit send.

He brings the hot water kettle over and pours some water on top of my used tea bag. Then he sits down and says, "Your mom says you don't need to know this, but I want to tell you what the Army chaplain said about your brother."

I set my phone on the table, but I don't let go. Touching it gives me a connection to the world beyond my family. After a minute I say, "Tell me. I want to know."

"I thought so. This is hard to hear, but you're not a little girl anymore." His words make me proud and I want to tell Bri, but I can't. "The Army told us an IED wiped out Brian's whole patrol; they found body parts but no survivors."

I cringe when he says "body parts." It's too ugly. Severed limbs and pools of blood. What does it feel like to be blown up?

"Three other soldiers had been found in the vicinity—or parts of them. The officer said the Army couldn't be sure how long they'd been lying in the open."

He swallows. I wait. He swallows again. Does he have as much of a lump in his throat as I do?

"Oh, honey," he finally says, dropping his military bearing. "There's no way to know what happened. We know he's not in pain, and we know he loved us, and maybe thinking of us kept him strong. The Army can't tell if he was killed instantly or he was alive when the body parts were severed."

I race to the bathroom. Vomit is tame next to severed body parts. I wash my face after I flush the toilet, but I can't stop crying. I'm trembling. I slip into my room and stare out the window at the neighborhood Bri will never see again.

Dad knocks on my door. "Honey? You okay?"

"I'll be out in a few minutes." I know this is hard on him, but I need to be alone. I reach for my phone, but it's still on the kitchen table. I sneak back to the kitchen, which is empty, grab my phone, go outside, and text four words to Tessa: "They found Bri's remains."

A minute later my phone rings. "Oh, Sandee, I'm so sorry." I nod violently.

"Can you talk?" she asks.

"Yes."

"What can you tell me?"

I explain about Jenn and Facebook, while I build up the courage to say that they're sending back body parts. "I can't stop imagining his pain."

"Don't." A second later she says, "I shouldn't tell you what to do, but what would Bri want you to do when you found out?"

"I don't know."

"What do you think?"

"I told you I don't know!"

"Why don't you make a list, okay?"

"Okay." I know she's trying to help.

"Send it to me anytime, and, Sandee, I'm truly sorry about the bad news."

I hang up, open the kitchen door, and listen. No one's around, so I go upstairs, grab my journal, and write.

What Bri Would Want Me To Do:
Get on with life.
Don't forget him.
Honor him in some way—or would he care about that?
Make him proud.
Contribute to the world in a way that matters to me.
Have fun.
Don't forget him!!!

Don't forget him says it all. Later, I call Tessa and read her my seven-point list. "I'm proud of you, Sandee." How long has it been since my parents told me they were proud of me? "You're still going to work on *Oklahoma*, aren't you?"

"You mean, 'The show must go on?'" I sound bitter, and I know it. Maybe I am. Is bitterness a part of grief?

"If you have tasks to accomplish, you have to concentrate, right?"

"I guess."

"That'll help you get on with life. What would you want Bri to do if your roles were reversed?"

"Get on with his life and make me proud," I say.

"You nailed it."

"Do you ever wish you could still send e-mails to Kayla?"

"I could, but there's not much point. That's why I'm keeping a journal. It's for when we can finally talk. I write about what's going on. I put in pictures. I tell her about the family and school and how much we love and miss her, and I tell her about the hero's welcome we're going to give her when she wakes up."

"You really know how to cope with this."

"It's either cope or surrender, and I'm not doing that."

I smile as we both hang up. This time it's a little easier to walk into the heavy silence inside our house.

On Monday I stay home. So do Mom and Dad. By the afternoon, I'm going stir crazy, so I ask Dad if he has any errands I can run. I need to get out of the house. He says I can walk to his office and pick up a couple of files if I promise not to read them. That sounds good to me.

Pale spring sunshine filters through the leafless trees that line the street. It feels good to walk in the sunshine. Bri will never walk down any street again.

I pass a mom who's jogging and pushing a baby carriage. A golden retriever runs next to her. I hope her husband isn't serving in the Armed Forces. She looks too happy to have her life ripped apart.

I pass Bake and Take, Generation to Generation, and the Valley Bank.

Then I come to the Stone Office Building. Somebody spray-painted a "d" on the end of Stone. Diego might have done something like that back in the seventh grade to leave his mark on the world. Stupid, I think as I go in.

Grayco Insurance is on the second floor, and Dad's receptionist is sealing an envelope as I walk in. Whatever it is, I won't have a chance to look, and I don't even care. The office has yellow walls with white trim. It's institutionally cheery, but I don't care today.

"So sorry about your loss," Dad's receptionist says when I walk in.

"Thanks." I take the sealed envelope from her. "This is everything he wants, right?"

"Yes, hon. Tell your dad we miss him, okay?"

"Sure." There's nothing else to say, so I leave.

I'm not ready to go home. I walk down the hall, looking at names on doors.

Smith & Hall, Attorneys at Law. Doctor Richard Mendelssohn, DDS. Doctor Robert Ramirez, PhD. – Psychological Evaluations. What would Doctor Ramirez find if he did a psychological evaluation on me right now?

A door marked *Private* swings open, and Nicole Lorca aka Ado Annie walks out of Dr. Ramirez's office. I have no idea what to say.

I don't have time to worry, though. She comes up to me and says, "I'm so sorry, Sandee. I can't imagine what it's like to lose a brother."

I'm glad she's ignoring Jenn's advice to leave me alone. I want to know what she's doing coming out of the private door of a shrink's office on a Monday afternoon and am about to ask one of those leading questions like the attorneys on TV shows when she says, "I guess you wonder what I'm doing here, right—or do you already know?"

She's beautiful, talented, and weird. "How would I know?"

"Rob didn't tell you why I miss so many rehearsals?" I see damp spots on the envelope. My hands are perspiring.

"No." I wish I could wipe my hands on something other than my jacket.

"I've got a few minutes before Mom picks me up. Let me buy you a coffee and explain."

We go next door to the Coffee Café and order two black coffees. I take mine off the counter and grab some sugar packets.

"Isn't one of those enough?" I've torn the tops off three of them and I'm pouring them all into my cup at once.

"Sugar makes me feel better." She rolls her eyes. I stop before the packets are empty and shove the excess to the edge of the table. "So, what are you doing here?" I ask.

"Seeing a shrink. It's part of my probation." She says it without emotion.

Did I hear her correctly? I stir the sugar into the coffee while my mind races.

"Probation?" I finally ask. "Does this have anything to do with why you weren't in *Harvey*?"

"You know how you drown your sorrows and frustrations in sugar? I used alcohol."

Wow! I'd never even considered that she might be a drinker. "You used alcohol?"

"Until I got busted," she says. "The police picked me up one night last July, probably about the time Bri went missing. I sang at Youth

Night. We were celebrating the new mural, I think. I don't really remember. I remember my solo, though. I struggled to reach the high notes, and afterwards, I told myself I'd missed a couple because my throat was sore. I'd had nothing but water all night, so as soon as I got offstage, I took a sip from a flask I used to carry in my backpack. It felt so good that I took another. Then I went outside so no one would see me. I missed the finale. I missed my curtain call. I told myself I didn't care.

"I watched all the families pouring out of the auditorium. When it looked like everybody had gone home, I started my car. I was barely out of the parking lot when I saw flashing lights in my rearview mirror. I rolled down my window, and the first thing the cop said was, 'Have you had anything to drink tonight?'

"'Of course not,' I said. 'I'm only sixteen.' Lying is what I did to protect myself back then. An officer with massive shoulders made me get out of the car, stuck a flashlight in my face, had me walk along one of the white lines of a parking space, and when I stumbled, he said, 'You're under arrest for a DUI.'"

My heart pounds. I can only imagine what hers must have done. I can't say anything, and maybe I'm not supposed to because she goes on like she can't hear the thumping in my chest.

"I don't think I was drunk, but that doesn't matter if you're sixteen. Any alcohol in your blood is too much, and when the Breathalyzer came back, it said I had 1.4, which is over the limit even if you're an adult. Long story short, the judge sentenced me to all kinds of community service, and she said I had to see a court-appointed shrink until I turn eighteen, and if I do everything they tell me, they'll seal my record when I'm twenty-one. That's what I want. Otherwise colleges and employers can find out I spent time in juvie. I don't ever want to go back there—not even for a night."

"So you were in juvie during *Harvey*?" I sound almost as ditzy as Jenn.

"Not exactly. I went to court in August, and the judge sent me to a ninety-day treatment program."

"Why are you telling me all this?"

"Did I tell you more than you wanted to know?"

I stir my coffee again, even though it's already half gone. I need something to do with my hands. "Not really," I finally say, and I mean it. "It explains a lot."

"When you have alcohol in your system, and you're only sixteen, you either go to juvie or go to rehab. Rehab sounded like summer camp compared to that hellhole, so I went. Little did I know their program would actually work."

"Pretty amazing."

"I want you to know because you're as dependent on sugar as I was on alcohol, and I don't want anything bad to happen to you—especially after you just lost Bri."

"Sugar's not illegal, and it doesn't mess with your head."

"No, but it ruins your health."

"Why are you trying to scare me?"

She shakes her head. "I'm trying to help. Eating sugar won't bring your brother back. Don't you want to be healthy?"

"Yes, but right now I want the sugar more."

"Exactly. You say you want it, but you believe you need it, don't you?"

She's right. I never thought of it this way before. I believe her, but I still don't want to hear it. Not today. Not when I need the sugar to help me cope. Who is she to lecture me? Sugar isn't as harmful as alcohol, but I know she's right about one thing: I depend on it to make me feel better.

"So, is Dr. Ramirez your therapist?" I ask to get her off the subject.

"Dr. Ramirez is supposed to follow me until I turn eighteen, which won't happen for another sixteen months. That means I can't go to NYU or Julliard for my freshman year. I'll be stuck at Pine

Mountain College if my parents don't make me work to pay back court costs and rehab." I take another sip of my sugary coffee. I can't figure out what to say. "Sugar and alcohol only make you feel better for a little while. Escaping isn't the answer."

That's why I came to Dad's office, though. I wanted to run an errand—any errand. I had to escape from that house and the misery it holds. "I don't try to escape every day. I only eat sugar because it tastes good."

She drinks the last of her coffee and says, "I want you to know you can call me instead of eating sweets or junk food. Especially if you think you're eating addictively. I have a ton of firsthand experience with consuming something to feel better."

Her phone beeps. "Mom's here. I've got to go. You can get my number off the call sheet, okay?"

"I'm not addicted to M&Ms, am I, Bri?" I ask after she's gone. I listen carefully, but he doesn't answer questions. He only talks to me when I'm not expecting him to.

CHAPTER SEVENTEEN

DEAR BRI,

I haven't written to you since you were away at camp and couldn't get e- mail. You were 11 and I was 8. Did I embarrass you? You never teased me about my long letters. Were you homesick and keeping it a secret?

Were you homesick in the Army? Were you scared the day you died?

Did you know you were going to die or did they shoot you from behind?

This feels weird. I'm not saying what I want to say. There's just so much I don't know. It bothers me, and I can't concentrate.

Do you ever have to concentrate in heaven? Are you in heaven?

Can you look down and see what's going on here?

If so, you know I miss you, right? I'm trying to go on. This semester that means working on our spring musical, Oklahoma!

I wanted to be in it more than you can imagine. I still do. Can you believe they picked Diego out of the orchestra and gave him a speaking role, and I didn't even get a part in *the chorus? There are more roles for boys than girls and they actually had to recruit boys for the chorus. Sometimes being a girl can be so unfair.*

I can hear you saying, "Talk to the teacher about it," just like Dad. Well I did. She said, "We're trying to do an authentic production of Oklahoma! *You wouldn't be believable as a man. You have too many curves." Can you believe it?*

So I'm the ASM. That's Assistant Stage Manager, and you'll never guess who the stage manager is. Come on. Guess.

Wait a minute. You don't have to guess, do you? You can look down and see him, right? Or can you? Will you ever even know I'm writing this?

If you can see from where you are, you know that the stage manager is your buddy, Rob. He's a senior now, and this is his last show, so maybe if I do good, I'll get to be the new stage manager after he's gone.

The ASM doesn't do much. So I asked Ms. G for a second job and she made me props manager because the girl who was supposed to do it quit. So I'm the only person who's assigned to two jobs, which is cool.

Then we got the news about you and everything changed.

Was it a gun that got you or a roadside bomb? Did you even know what hit you? I can't imagine being here one minute and on the other side the next. What is that like? Can you find a way to tell me? There must be a way.

You remember when Nana died? Mom told me that she asked Nana to let her know if there was an afterlife. So on Nana's birthday Mom went to a computer class at the community center. She sat in the last row, and when she touched the mouse, a screen came up, only it wasn't the community center's regular screen. The background was chalkboard green, and in this perfect cursive she read the words, "Hello, Susan." They looked like they were written in the same chalk Nana used in Room 9 all those years she taught fourth grade.

Mom wondered how the tech staff knew where she'd sit, and how they'd programmed the computer to do this. She looked at as many other computers as she could, but they all had the community center logo on them, and their users were texting or chatting as if everything was normal.

She kept staring at her message, "Hello, Susan," and trying to figure out what the computer techs had done.

About a week later, she was thinking about it as she drove to work, and that's when she realized that Nana's message appeared on her birthday, to let Mom know it was really her. Like code.

So if you want to send me code to let me know you're okay and there is another side, I'd love to get it. On your birthday or any day. On my computer or on my iPhone. Just find a way, okay?

You are someplace, aren't you? You're not lingering here like they talked about in the old movie Ghost, *are you?*

Do you feel safe now? I don't anymore. I know you were prepared to die when you went to war, but I've become conscious of traffic deaths and airplane crashes and all the other ways fate interferes with our lives and our plans. I don't feel like I have control anymore.

Mom and Dad are trying to cope, so they're fine one minute and weird the next. When they look at me, I'm always afraid they're thinking, "Why can't you be like Bri? He was successful. When are you going to be a success?" Maybe I'm just being paranoid.

They took me to a support group right before we got the news about you.

You didn't tell them to try that, did you?

Did you?

Did you suggest it in a dream or something?

While we were there, I met this really cool senior named Tessa. Her sister was in Afghanistan, just like you, but she got sent home with a TBI. Her name's Kayla. Did you know her?

ANSWER ME, okay? I think you're out there somewhere, and I hope this reaches you somehow. I'd send this if I could, but if I put Brian Mason, US Army Specialist, Heaven somebody might see it and call Mom or Dad.

Did I tell you we love you and miss you? We do.

Love from your sister (I am still your sister, even if you're not here, aren't I?),

Sandee

I put it in my "Saved" folder. Then I change my mind and print it out. I fold it and put it in my backpack. I start to go downstairs, but instead, I take the letter out of my backpack and hide it in a shoebox in the back of my closet. I delete the e-mail and empty the trash. I don't want anyone to think I'm crazy. It's for Bri's eyes only. I don't even want Tessa to see it.

CHAPTER EIGHTEEN

DAD SAYS I CAN stay home all week. By Thursday, I can't stand the gloom. "Do you think I could go to rehearsal?" I ask him, while Mom sits at the kitchen table staring at the grain in the wood. "If I don't get out of here, I'll go crazy."

Dad calls Ms. G, who says she'll be happy to have me back whether I've attended class or not. So here I stand at the edge of the parking lot right before the end of seventh period, staring at the shadows of leaves and tree branches on the silent buildings. The rehearsal room is half-hidden behind oaks that are older than God.

Inside, Ms. G is helping people with scenes or maybe doing an acting exercise with the whole class, and everybody is waiting for the bell. How many times did Bri wait for that bell? "I'm so sorry, Bri," I whisper as I stare at the campus.

"It's going to be okay," I imagine him saying. I know it's my imagination, because the voice inside my head sounds like me.

Have I ever heard his voice? Really heard it—or did I only want to believe? I'd love to talk to a psychic about it. It beats talking to a shrink like Nicole's forced to do.

The wind swept the sky clean and clear, and the trees on campus shimmer in the sunlight. I walked across campus as quietly as a ghost. Is Bri a ghost now? Does his spirit come here to check on his alma mater or go to Berkeley to check on Emma—or come by the house to see how his family is doing without him?

"Stop!" I say out loud. My voice ripples across the quad, but no one comes out to ask what all the noise is about, so maybe I only think I hear myself.

When I walk towards the rehearsal room, Rob takes me aside and tells me the whole cast is thinking about Bri, which is weird because Bri didn't hang with the drama or band kids. Maybe he means they're thinking about me?

Then he says, "You'll never believe it, Sandee, but I found some old guns that might be perfect for the show. I don't know if they can pass for the ones that cowboys used back in the day, so I need you to check them against the history book." He hands me a slip of paper with a name and address. "They belong to Jeff Gregory."

"The old Army major who yells if a dog pees in his yard?"

"That's the one. He's not as scary as we used to think, and he didn't remember the firecrackers that Bri and I put in his mailbox back when we were kids. Besides, I think he's got Alzheimer's or something, so just pick up the guns, okay?"

I take the scrap of paper with his address on it and say, "El Brasero Avenue? That's practically across the street."

"So you can walk it, right?"

"Absolutely, but I need to check in with Ms. G first."

He shakes his head, and I noticed five hairs sprouting from his chin. "I'll tell her you showed up, and I sent you to check the guns."

"Do you have a copy of the letter he's supposed to sign?"

"Already handled. Just take your history book so you can make sure they look right, and if they do, stash them in this duffel bag so the police don't pick you up. The last thing we need is trouble."

"Okay. You're the boss."

He grins. "Good to have you back."

I knock on the Gregory's door, but no one answers. I knock louder. Nothing. Further down the porch I see a window and peer in. A gruff voice says, "Can I help you with something, or should I call the police?"

"I'm sorry. No one answered the doorbell."

"What do you want?"

"I'm here about the guns you offered San Ramos Drama."

"What happened to the boy who came by on Tuesday?"

"He's the stage manager, and he's at rehearsal." I show him my student ID and follow him on the brick path leading to his garage.

"He's in the show? He could barely talk."

That doesn't sound like Rob. Maybe he was having a bad day, or maybe Bri's death has gotten to him too.

Gregory's mellower than the guy who used to yell at Bri and Rob, but he's off in his own little world. He unlocks the garage door and flips on a light switch. I follow him to a workbench where three revolvers and two rifles are laid out.

"This what you need?"

I reach out, but I shudder. I can't touch a gun. Any gun. Not even a disabled one. Not after what happened to Bri. So I flip to a flagged page in *The American Vision*, compare the two and say, "They look real to me."

"They are." We both stand in silence for a moment, staring at them. "They were," he adds without taking his eyes off them. "I disabled them so my daughter would bring my grandson around. He's a cute little bugger, but he grabs everything. I never put the firing pins back in."

With great effort, I pick up a wooden-handled pistol and hold its sleek, black barrel in my hand. It's cold. It's nothing. It's everything. I get so confused.

What kind of gun did the Army issue Bri? He would have used it if he needed to, so I figure his patrol ran into a roadside bomb or was ambushed. No way anybody can look in all directions at once.

"So, will these work for your show, missy?" he asks again.

I set the gun on his wooden workbench and say, "My name's Sandee."

"Right, missy."

"Yep, and you're Jeff Gregory," I say without thinking how it might sound to him.

"Major Gregory." It comes out as a command.

"Which war?"

"The Misunderstood War." I must look puzzled because he adds, "Vietnam—but these were my grandfather's. He collected some from the sons and grandsons of Texas cowboys and took others off dead soldiers in World War II. I don't think your audience will know the difference. Every generation in our family served in the Army."

"Mine too," I say quietly.

"You going in when you turn eighteen? You could be a communication specialist or an ambulance driver."

I shake my head. "Your guns look right to me." I stuff them into the duffel bag Rob handed me when he met me outside the rehearsal room. "How much do they weigh?" I ask.

Instead of giving me a weight, he says, "You might be strong enough. You don't look as wimpy as the girls in swishy little skirts who live up the street." He doesn't say they're too heavy for a girl, and I love that.

"Do you have a copy of the contract that Rob had you sign, just so I can take it to the drama teacher?"

"What contract?"

"The one from the teacher that asks you to guarantee they're disabled."

"You don't need a contract. I gave you my word. They're disabled. So I could see my grandson. Do you want them or not?"

"Of course I want them." I know, though, that I need his word in writing. "Can I write something out and have you sign it?"

"I know they're disabled, and I'll write my own note for the teacher," Major Gregory barks. He flips moods faster than a rock star on cocaine. "What's his name?"

"Ms. Gittinger."

He snorts, but he writes something on a piece of paper, folds it, and hands it to me. I unfold it, and he shouts, "You don't need to read that."

"Why shouldn't I?"

"It's for your teacher. I'm not sure why that boy sent you. A girl shouldn't be carrying guns."

Total turnaround. Maybe Rob was right about the Alzheimer's. I pick up the duffel bag. It's heavy, but I can handle it. "Thanks for helping us out."

He's sort of like Nana. She had dementia, and at the end, she could never remember my name or Bri's. Did Bri see her when he got to heaven? Does heaven really exist?

In the theater, almost every actor is onstage, but only half of them are in character. I hoist the duffel bag onto Ms. G's desk and stand there while Diego calls, "Line." Rob gives it to him, and he repeats it. His deadpan delivery sucks. If he doesn't want the role, they should make me Corletta Elam. I can be Aunt Eller's cook. I can even cook for the cowboys, and that would give me a reason to hang out with them. This is good. Maybe I should take up playwriting.

Ms. G says, "You all have fifteen minutes to find a partner and run lines. Principals pair up with chorus members. Engage your brains and your characters' hearts. Any questions?"

Diego stares at the stage floor.

"'Lines due' has been on the schedule for four weeks," Ms. G adds as the cast breaks into partners. Nicole goes over, takes Diego's arm as if she were still Ado Annie, and leads him backstage. He's lucky to have her expertise, and I'm lucky Jenn doesn't march between the two of them and shove her out of the way.

"We're glad you're back, Sandee," Ms. G says as I unzip the duffel bag.

"Major Gregory sent you a note saying these are disabled." I hand it to her. "I guess he lost the contract Rob gave him."

"Okay. Lock them up. We'll get somebody to check them before we put them in the actors' hands," she says in her no-nonsense voice.

"I'll check them, Ms. G." Rob has taken off his North Face jacket, and his brown plaid shirt brings out the color of his eyes.

"No, Rob. You're a student, and how could he have lost the contract you gave him? Didn't you explain we're a school, and it's essential that any weapons—"

He cut her off. "Gregory's an old geezer. He forgot. I gave him your contract, and I watched him sign it. I swear."

"Okay. Rob, please lock these in the props cabinet. Put them on the back of the bottom shelf, and be sure you return the keys to my hand. Sandee, do you want to look up the high schools that have done *Oklahoma!* in the last three years and see if any of them still have a surrey or at least the base? You can use the computer on my desk."

I scroll through the pages, and find three high schools within twenty-five miles that have *Oklahoma!* listed on their drama web page. One is a magnet school in Oakland, one is a public high school in Walnut Creek, and the third is a private prep school with campuses in Lafayette and Berkeley.

I have just finished leaving a message at the magnet school when Jenn comes over and whispers, "Were you at home when the Army came to your house on Saturday?"

"No. I was here. Even you were here by then."

Her face is blank. "You don't mind what I posted on Facebook, do you?"

"Isn't it a little late to ask?"

"I thought it would be better if people knew. We all cared about Bri, Sandee. We care about you too. I wanted to make things easier for you."

"Did you even know Bri?"

"I knew *about* him. Everybody knew about him once he disappeared. What is your problem?"

"No problem." I don't mean it. "It's not like you can print a retraction any more than I can bring him back."

Her eyes grow wide, and she looks like I threw up on her. "I'm sorry he's gone, Sandee, but you don't have to be such a bitch about it. Should you even be here?"

Rob calls, "Five minutes," which cuts her off, and she goes backstage without another word. He repeats the same call to the people running lines outside under the old oak. I ask myself why Jenn isn't running lines before I remember she only has two.

I can't believe her. I have responsibilities to this show, just like Bri has responsibilities over in Afghanistan. *Had.* This is a lot safer. A Facebook post is nothing compared to what he went through. I am here to honor my brother and help the show—not cater to her ego.

I catch sight of Diego out of the corner of my eye. He's talking to Jenn. When the rehearsal starts again, he stares at me with the same astonished look Jenn did. I slink further down in my seat.

I'm not the one who put the post on Facebook. I'm the one who lost her brother. Why should I feel guilty?

CHAPTER NINETEEN

DIEGO MEETS HIS MATH tutor after rehearsal, so I start home alone. Rob pulls up next to me, rolls down the window and says, "Need a lift?"

As I get in, I notice a new rip in the upholstery. Rob doesn't say anything about it, and I don't ask, but I wonder what happened. I stow my backpack on the floorboard and tell Rob, "In three more weeks, I'll have my own license."

"When did you finish Driver's Training?" he asks without taking his eyes off the road.

"Right before auditions. Maybe my parents will give me Bri's old car."

He pulls up to the curb. We're still in downtown San Ramos. "Want to try driving a Honda?"

My heart flips in my chest. "Do you mean it? Right now?"

"Give it a shot," he said with the flirty grin I love. "You're a big girl."

"How rude!"

The minute I say it, he reaches over the console, puts his hand on my shoulder, and says, "Why do you take compliments the wrong way? You're a lovely, curvaceous fox, and I thought you might like a chance to drive something other than your dad's ten-year-old Camry. Besides, you picked up the guns for me, and now it's my turn to do something nice for you."

I giggle. I can't help it. He's so self-righteous and sincere and gutsy all at once. He's cute and cool and normal and everything Bri will never be again. I can't stop laughing, even when he says, "It's not a joke." I laugh harder and harder until the laughs turn into gasps.

With no warning, the gasps turn into sobs. I can't catch my breath. Rob puts his arms around me until the sobs slow down. Then he strokes my cheek. I look into his eyes. "Better?"

I smile. At least I try to.

He turns my face towards him and kisses me. His lips are warm and gentle and soft. Then he kisses me harder, and his tongue reaches for mine, sending an unexpected hunger through my body. When he's done, he releases me and says, "It's about time."

"What do you mean?"

He presses his index finger into my lips. "You've been through a horrible shock, and this is much more real than your silence on Saturday."

I draw in a shaky breath and wipe the tears off my face.

He holds my hand in both of his. "Take a deep breath. You're going to be okay."

"I know. I need to talk about something else." I reach into my backpack, find an old Kleenex. He's silent. It's up to me to change the subject. "So can I still drive?"

"If you want to." We trade places, and I look around to make sure that no one sees me getting into his driver's seat. I'm not supposed to drive with someone who's not eighteen, but I can't turn this down. Besides, we're only six blocks from my house. I buckle my seatbelt and check the mirrors. I turn the key in the ignition, put it in reverse, look in all mirrors, and pull out slowly.

Once I'm in the street, I say, "Tell me what I missed this week."

"Not much. We've been working scenes and running them, working the transitions into songs, and adding some choreography. The light plot's ready, but that's not what you want to know is it?"

"No."

"Tessa's been covering for you on props. Jenn's been flirting with Diego and distracting him onstage. Nicole hasn't missed a rehearsal all week, and that's some kind of a record."

"Why can't you guys give her a second chance?" He looks over. I squirm, but I don't take my eyes off the road.

"How do you know she needs one?"

"She told me where she was when *Harvey* was cast. Don't you think it was gutsy of her to come back to school here?"

"If you think any of us are going to feel sorry for her, think again. What she did was stupid."

"Yeah, but she paid for it," I say, looking at him. He points at the road, and I turn my head back. After a minute I ask, "Why are you so mean to her?"

"How do you think Jenn felt when the role of Ado Annie went to Nicole? It could have been hers."

Even though I see his point, I say, "Nicole is the better actress."

"Unless she screws up and misses opening night."

"Has she ever missed an opening?"

I see him shaking his head through my peripheral vision. Even though I'm at a stoplight, I won't take my eyes off the road long enough to look over. The last thing I need is to have an accident before I even get my license.

"I guess you're right. She won't miss a chance to perform. It would be too much of a blow to her ego," Rob says after the light changes. "But what if she shows up drunk?"

I put my foot on the gas and start through the intersection. "Look, I don't know what she was like before, but she's trying to graduate next year and move on to Pine Mountain, since she can't go away."

When I mention Pine Mountain, he licks his lips and says, "That's another thing that happened while you were gone. Jenn said that a scout from Pine Mountain's drama department is coming to the show."

My heart flutters. "Are you kidding me? Pine Mountain is looking for high school talent?"

"Apparently, they're looking for young talent for their summer repertory season, and they went to the children's theater. Jenn's mom told them to visit the high schools—especially San Ramos. I'm sure Nicole doesn't want to blow her chances."

I'll only be onstage to change the props, but maybe they'll be impressed with all the authentic looking things I've brought in. Maybe they'll want me to do props for them. Of course I'd rather have a role, but maybe something will happen and they'll need someone to step in, like Carmen in *Sisterhood of the Traveling Pants 2*. How great would it be to hang out with college kids all summer? I'm not about to share my dream just yet, so I flip my hair back and ask, "Anything else?"

"Monday morning Dr. Henderson made an announcement about Bri at the end of Morning Messages. He said a recent graduate, Brian Mason, died heroically during a battle in Afghanistan. Then he asked for a moment of silence. Between that and Jenn's message on Facebook, everybody knows, but probably half of them have forgotten, knowing the kids in this school."

I pull into my driveway slowly, turn off the engine, and set the parking brake. I can't believe I'm this sleepy. I lower the visor and look in the mirror. My face is a blotchy mess. "Did you really mean it when you said I was a 'curvaceous fox'?"

"As much as I meant that kiss. The minute I saw you at auditions, I hoped we'd be a couple by opening night."

I grin. Then Diego's face pops into my head. "You're too much. On Saturday you were treating me like a sister and now I'm a fox?"

"You are many things, and I was trying to step in for a missing buddy on Saturday. I think he'd be pleased that we're a couple." He kisses me again, much quicker this time, and says, "I won't be at school tomorrow, so you'll be holding the book."

"Where are you going?"

"Field trip. Call me later." I know Tessa doesn't think much of Rob, but how would Bri feel about my dating him? Why did he tell me we were a couple instead of asking me if I wanted to be his girlfriend?

CHAPTER TWENTY

ON FRIDAY, WE HAVE a rally to get us stoked for the basketball game. Diego's a drummer, so he sits with the band. Jenn and I are both sophomores, but she sits with her skinny choir friends. I huddle alone on the end of the bleachers and pretend I'm invisible. It's the only way to get through all the cheering and screaming.

We'll be playing our archrivals, Mountain View. Most of the drama kids won't go. They'll be at Rob's, unless he's not back from his field trip.

Not me, though. I haven't been to a party at Rob's since that first night. Diego says I got drunk. It scares me that I can't remember the ride home. If I was so drunk, why didn't his dad tell my dad? I'm glad he didn't, but, really, how did I get so lucky? The whole thing doesn't make sense. I like to stay in control. Rob does too. He's a master of control, so it's odd that he likes to drink so much, unless it doesn't affect him like it did me. I don't ever want to be hungover again.

It would be fun to take BART to Berkeley, see a movie, and grab something at one of the Chinese restaurants on Shattuck tonight. We'd have such a good time we wouldn't even need alcohol. Maybe I'll suggest it at rehearsal.

Five cheerleaders all shout, "J-U-M-P. JUMP IT UP!" I'm not into basketball any more than they're into drama, but they remind me of the chorus in *Oklahoma!* as they chant together.

That afternoon at rehearsal, Ms. G tells me that the drama teacher at Oakland Magnet's performing arts department borrowed their surrey base from the Rockinghorse Ranch on the west side of Pine Mountain. They'll rent us the supports and their fringed cover for $50 a night. All we have to do is pick them up and return them right after we close. "Rob and I can handle it," I promise even though I'm not sure whether he can borrow a truck that weekend.

Ms. G gives me the address of the ranch, which is on Diablo Road. Then she says, "Rob's on a field trip, so you'll hold the prompt book today. Give them a line if they ask, but don't offer it unless they call for it, okay?"

"Sure."

Only three actors say "Line" all afternoon. Diego isn't one of them, and I'm proud of him.

We take a break at 4:30, and the actors are already texting and checking messages when Jenn calls out, "Hey, everybody, the talent scouts from Pine Mountain College will be here in three weeks. Remember we want to shine onstage."

"We already know," the actor playing Will Parker says at the same moment the question "What about those of us offstage?" flashes through my head. I don't say that. Instead I call out, "One more announcement: If anybody'd like to see a *Les Mis* revival at the Shattuck in Berkeley tonight, meet at the bus stop in front of the school at 6:15. We'll take the 6:20 bus to BART. Show starts at 8:10."

"Is this from you or from Rob?" the blond-haired boy playing Curley asks.

He stares at me like he can't believe I'm taking the initiative. "It's from me, but I'll invite Rob."

He gives me a weird look, nodding and rolling his eyes at the same time, but he doesn't say anything.

Several of the seniors laugh, and one of them says, "I think Rob's got other plans." Someone I don't know looks over at Ms. G and tries to shush him, but Ms. G's talking on her cell. She has already dismissed us, and most of the kids are putting on jackets, picking up backpacks, and heading out the door.

A few singers hang out by the piano singing "Nothing Like Us." Jenn accompanies them. I text Tessa. "Going to Les Mis in Berkeley tonight. Want 2 come?"

She writes back, "No drama party?"

"Instead."

"Terrific idea, Sandee. I have a support group meeting tonight, but maybe I can get out of it. Want me to drive?"

"Taking BART."

"Excellent."

I look around the theater to see if anyone else is interested. Nicole might be. She's going over her script, though she knows every line. No way she's going to drink to take away the pain, unlike the guy in the song everyone's singing.

The sun, a flaming ball of gold, is sinking below Las Trampas Ridge when Nicole joins Diego and me at the bus stop. "Where's everybody else?" Diego asks.

"Some are partying with Rob, I suppose," Nicole says, tugging on a brown leather boot. "Some are prepping for Mock Trial. Some are going to the Mountain View game, and maybe some have parents who won't let them go to Berkeley on a Friday night."

"Wow. You've thought of everything."

"I know my high school cliques. I've been through enough of them to last a lifetime."

"Which ones?" Diego asks.

"Leave the girl alone," I say, elbowing his arm. I know it's silly. He shoves me back, and I giggle. I'm not sure why.

"She's trying to distract me," Diego says to Nicole. "Tell me everything about high school cliques. Can you do it in one night?"

I jab him harder. Why can't he take a hint? "We're glad you're here, Nicole. Diego just has an odd way of showing it."

"Since when?" he asks as Tessa pulls up. She rolls down her window and asks, "Is this all of you?"

"Yup. The few, the proud . . . Never mind," Diego says.

"If no one else comes, let's take my car." The bus rolls by a couple minutes later, and Diego and I step back, bow deeply like we're taking our curtain call, and wave. The driver probably wonders what we're doing, and some of the passengers stare, but Diego and I are laughing too hard to care.

We hop into Tessa's car, and she looks behind her before she pulls away from the curb. I look over at Nicole, who's sitting beside Tessa. "Texting my parents," she says. "No offense, Tessa. They think it makes me trustworthy." She turns and says, "You two should do the same thing," so Diego and I both do, even though I feel silly. Diego shows me his dad's response, "Thx." A minute later, my dad texts "10/4." I don't think they know we're together, and we start to laugh again. Nicole leans over to Tessa and whispers, "First love." I feel my cheeks flaming, but I don't deny it, even though I'm not sure Diego feels the same way I do.

We turn onto 24 outside Walnut Creek and get off on Telegraph in Oakland. A violet neon sign in the window of a small, white house flashes the word *psychic*. "Ever wonder if that psychic stuff works?" I ask over the song playing on KROK.

Nobody answers. Maybe nobody heard. Maybe that's a good thing, because I squirm as I ask, and if my own question makes me squirm, I have my answer. I reach for the M&Ms in my backpack and as I pull them out Diego says, "Don't you ever go anywhere without those things?"

"Of course I do."

Nicole ignores us, but I'm sure she knows what he's talking about.

Diego puts his hand in mine. I let him keep me from my candy and smile. "Too bad Jenn couldn't come too," I say, just to see what he'll say back.

He shakes his head. "If it won't help her get into the Pine Mountain Summer Festival, she's not interested."

Tessa parks near the Shattuck Cinemas, and Diego holds my hand again as we walk towards the box office. We pass a homeless guy with a dirty face, a scruffy dog, and an open guitar case. "Glad I'm not him," Diego says. I agree.

The music in *Les Mis* is gorgeous; it swells around us and practically swallows us up. How could anybody not love this show? It's supposed to be about injustice and the French Revolution, but it's really about love. This is way better than whatever is going on at Rob's house.

After the show, we stop at Mel's, which is next to the theater. Diego and I split a plate of French fries. Neither one of us thought to bring money for food. I can't stop smiling at Diego. He's not paying any attention to either Nicole or Tessa, and the two of them keep chatting about shows and art, and nobody talks about school or San Ramos, and for the first time since we got the news about Bri, I'm free of stress.

As Diego and I get into the back seat of Tessa's car after we leave Mel's, I see a girl who looks a lot like Bri's Emma, but it can't be her because she's in a lip-lock with some guy in a pea jacket who wears glasses. Reminders of Bri pop up when I least expect them, but tonight I'm too happy to get upset.

We drive home talking about Fantine's acting and the exquisite singing and how impossible it would be to do a show like that at San Ramos High. I imagine doing "I Dreamed a Dream" as a monologue for Ms. G's class. I'd be as intense and desperate as Anne Hathaway, and after the comments were over, I'd say, "If you want to do the whole show, I'd love to play Fantine." It probably wouldn't work, but I can dream.

Before I know it, we're passing Lafayette BART, and I stare at the brightly lit hill of crosses honoring veterans of the Iraq War. Will we put up one for Bri?

Tessa sighs loudly. She's probably thinking about Kayla. There are no memorials for those who lie in a coma.

"Do you suppose there's always a war somewhere?" I ask.

"Pretty much," Tessa says.

"There are all kinds of wars," Nicole says to the darkened windshield, and I'm sure she's thinking of her own battle with alcohol. "Life doesn't stop when people get injured or go missing, and nobody plans to get captured or die. I support our troops, but sometimes I think war's a silly waste of life and talent."

I've never heard her say anything like that. Have the war scenes in *Les Mis* made her think that, or am I getting to know her better?

I jump when my cell beeps. It's Rob. "Too late to see *Les Mis*," his text says. "Come over if you have time."

I read it to everyone in the car and then type, "Can we pick up surrey tomorrow?" Diego and Nicole are still laughing at the way I ignored his invitation when I hit send.

"Busy. Call u in an hour."

I read that to everyone in the car too, and Nicole says, "Typical."

CHAPTER TWENTY-ONE

TESSA DRIVES US ALL the way home. Diego and I get out together, and I ask, "Coming over?" Just as I do, his dad texts, "Coming in?"

He shows it to me; we laugh, and he says, "Have fun picking up the surrey with Rob." He goes past the little path lights that line his family's brick sidewalk and disappears inside his house.

I'm in the living room staring at a taped episode of *Ravenswood*, a TV show about the supernatural, when my cell rings. Rob says he'll give me a ride and then says, "I'll be driving Uncle Sam's pickup, so wear grubbies. He never bothers to clean it."

"Uncle Sam? Really?"

"Mom's brother."

Uncle Sam is an American icon, I want to scream at him, but I'm an Army daughter, and he's used to thinking of a relative when he says "Uncle Sam."

"I'll pick you up around ten." He ends the call before I can tell him I'll wait out front. It doesn't matter. He'll see me.

In the morning I put on my workday cords and a flannel shirt over a navy long-sleeved tee. I add boots and my Rainforest Café jacket. When I see myself in the mirror, I add a bit of lip gloss and mascara. A little makeup looks good.

Not that it matters. Last night Diego and I were holding hands. They can't both be my boyfriend, and I don't want all this confusion, but I love my shimmery, sexy lips.

Mom's slumped in front of a Lifetime movie. They play all day on Saturday. I grab my backpack from the table next to the front door and say, "I'm going out."

Ten seconds later, my cell rings. "Where are you going?" Mom asks. I'm still on the porch.

Even though her depression is intense, she's trying to be a mom, so I explain that Rob and I are picking up the surrey base, and we'll be back soon. "Don't worry so much," I say, though it never registers. All she does is sit in front of the TV and stare. She hasn't been to work since we heard about Bri's death.

There. I said the word. Death. Dad says her depression has intensified, but she refuses to talk to a shrink. Tessa says I can't change Mom; I can only change myself, but what I really want to do is change how others see me.

Rob pulls up in "Uncle Sam's" brown pickup. I know nothing about trucks, so he uses an I'm-smarter-than-you tone as he explains, "It's a Ford F-250." I don't really care what it is as long as it can haul the surrey base. I give him the address of the Rockinghorse Ranch on Diablo Road, and he puts it in his GPS.

As we start up Pine Mountain, I see tiny green bumps on the tree branches. They'll be baby leaves by the time the show opens. They cling tightly even though the wind whooshes. They're like our cast and Bri's platoon. Follow the script. Follow orders. Keep track of your props. Keep track of your gun.

Overhead, billowy clouds hang in an azure sky, oblivious to my obsessive need to make everything correlate.

"The cast should come up here and get a feel for what open country is like, except I don't think there are a lot of mountains in Oklahoma. I could Google it."

"We've got three weeks until we open, Sandee, and we have more important things to do."

"Don't be a grouch," I say. He keeps his eyes on the road and his hands on the steering wheel. We ride in silence until I ask, "Is something wrong?"

He reaches over and puts his hand on my knee. I wasn't expecting that. "Where were you last night?"

"I told you that a bunch of us went to Berkeley and saw *Les Mis.*"

"A bunch of you?"

"A few. I announced it last minute, so only Diego, Nicole, and I could go—and Tessa."

He rolls his eyes when I mention her name. "Why did you drag Tessa into it?"

"She's a part of the show, and it was for the whole cast, just like your parties. Why don't you like her?"

"She acts all high and mighty," he says as we round a hairpin curve so fast that we lurch. "It bugs a lot of the seniors."

"Sorry, but we had a good time and saw a wonderful movie." Why did I say I'm sorry? I'm sick of being sorry about everything.

He swings around the next curve with so much speed that the tires squeal when he slams on the brakes. Once he straightens the truck out he says, "Most of us stick together when we're doing a show. The parties are a tradition, and if people don't show up, they make themselves outcasts. We watched the *Rocky Horror Picture Show* and acted out parts, just like they do at the midnight shows in the city. It was a blast. Loosen up and let us like you."

I don't want to loosen up the way they do, but if I say so, Rob will treat me like a kid again. I know everybody drinks, but I don't like the hangover.

I like the way Rob kissed me that night, though, and I like the way he kissed me in the car after rehearsal. That felt so good! Diego only holds hands.

"You okay?" he asks because I don't say anything about loosening up.

"Just watching for the . . . There it is. There's Rockinghorse Ranch."

Smooth, whitewashed logs frame a dirt road with tire tracks sunk into the dust. A Rockinghorse Ranch sign hangs above the entrance, swinging on rusty hooks.

Rob drives past overgrown pastures filled with thistles and wildflowers until we see a sprawling, ramshackle place.

"What a mess." His tires crunch on the dried weeds. The road goes past a big house with peeling paint and a boarded window on the second floor. Mom would say it looks "lived in."

An old man with leathery skin comes off the dusty porch of the caretaker's cottage. He peers through the driver's window and says, "Howdy, I'm Chuck. Chuck Williams." He looks past Rob and asks, "You Sandee Mason?"

"Absolutely." I reach past Rob's chest to shake his extended hand. "Rob's our stage manager as well as the driver."

"You've already loaned this to another production, right?" Rob asks.

"Yeah. You going to offer my boss free advertising like the last school did?"

"We can do that. What do you want to advertise?" Rob asks before I can open my mouth.

"The boss owns Fresh Veggies down on San Ramos Road. I'll have him e-mail you his ad, okay?"

I hand Chuck a sheet with the ad information, and he leads us to the barn. "Stuff's been gatherin' dust for decades," he says as he pulls the barn door along its rusty track. It squeaks. "I don't know why the boss is holding on to all this junk. He'll never turn this back into a working ranch. He's too tight to hire the help he needs."

The "junk" is old lanterns, buckets, horseshoes, bridles, saddles, hoes, rakes, and rusty farming equipment. It's a props collector's dream.

"You don't sound like you're from around here," I say as Rob pulls a stack of splintery wooden fence posts out of the way.

"Fact is, I'm originally from Oklahoma," Chuck says as he gives

Rob a hand. "That's the reason I want to help out. I love that you kids are doin' that show."

"Awesome."

Rob rolls his eyes. I don't know why.

"Is Oklahoma like it was in the olden days?"

"Maybe in a few places. My grandpa told me there was a time when you could ride the prairies for days and see nuthin' but cattle and horses and other cowboys. At night, you'd make camp, picket the horses, and stretch out around a campfire. No women folks to fancy things up, according to the old-timers, but they must all be dead by now. Oklahoma's got city and country, just like here. Not as many of them fancy restaurants, though."

"In the show, Will Parker goes to the city."

"That'd be Tulsa, I expect." Chuck looks like an old cowboy with a piece of straw hanging from his mouth. "Here you are, little lady. If you like it, we'll haul it out." Chuck and Rob each take one of the poles that extend in front, and they wheel out an ebony surrey base, complete with old wooden wheels and a long tongue. It's perfect.

I let the two of them haul it up into the back of the truck even though I can tell Rob's getting pissed. "Let her help. That's what she's here for," he says, but Chuck shakes his head.

"Good job," I say as they get it on the bed and secure it with rope. On Monday we'll pick up the frame and cover in Oakland. I considered bringing an extra $100 with me in case I could persuade Rob to stop at the psychic shop on Telegraph, but I still need to check out the psychic who works there.

We climb back into the cab and are headed down the mountain when I say, "Do you ever get a feeling about something before it happens?"

"What are you talking about, Sandee?" Rob asks as he downshifts.

"Never mind. Just something I read in a magazine quiz," I lie. Something in his tone stops me from asking what he thinks about psychics.

He turns on Uncle Sam's radio. Some woman whose name I don't know sings an oldie called "I Never Promised You a Rose Garden," and when she sings "Along with the sunshine/There's got to be a little rain sometime" I feel tears welling up again.

(HAPTER TWENTY-TWO

WHEN ROB TURNS INTO our driveway, the sycamores cast long shadows, and the wind whips them to and fro. "You don't want to come in, do you?" I ask.

"Well, when you put it that way. . . "

The look in his eyes makes me realize I'm being rude. "Sorry. Moving that surrey was hard work. You want a Coke?"

"Another time. I've got to meet somebody."

"You sure?"

He nods and smiles. I think he's eager to go, but I have one more question. "Do you think the surrey will be safe backstage?"

Earlier, we drove up to the rehearsal room just before Ms. G was about to lock it.

Rob asked her for the key to the auditorium. She came over with us, and they showed me how to pull out a special ramp that leads into the loading doors backstage. Then Rob and Diego hauled it up the ramp while Ms. G and I pushed from behind. Nicole helped too, while Jenn stood around saying, "You guys are so strong."

We left it behind the traveler, which masks the backstage area, and Ms. G gave us a roll of caution tape to put around it so the community groups would know they should leave it alone. She told us that the back half of the stage was reserved for drama from now until two days after closing, but still I worry.

"You're starting to get frown lines, and you're not even sixteen," Rob says outside my house, but he's grinning, and that makes me smile.

"I will be on Monday, March 27. You know I couldn't have done this without you, don't you?"

"Maybe someday you'll pay me back. Are you feeling better today, Sandee?"

I've been concentrating on other things all day, but his question brings the loss of Bri right back. "I've got to go in," I say, and he nods like he knows that I don't want to talk about it.

"You know I miss him too."

"I know." I watch him back Uncle Sam's truck up through the tears swimming in my eyes. When will I stop crying?

Once he's out of sight, I dig into my backpack and fortify myself with a handful of M&Ms before going into the house. The TV's blaring, but Mom isn't on the sofa. She isn't in the kitchen. "Mom?" I call out. My voice bounces against the walls. "Mom, can you hear me?"

"Over here." She's staring at a battered green footlocker with *MASON—U.S. ARMY* stenciled on it. She holds a glass of wine in her hand.

We stare at it together. She can't stop crying, just like me the other day. I stroke the footlocker. She cries harder. "Do you want me to call Dad, or should you and I do this together?" I finally ask.

"It must be terrible to come home and find your mother drinking in the middle of the day."

Okay. She can't answer my question. For a second I almost ask for a sip of her wine, but instead I say, "If I were you, I'd drink too."

She stops crying and looks into my eyes. "You don't, do you?"

"Of course not." She doesn't know about Rob's party, and I haven't had anything since then. "Give me the key. I'll open it up, and we'll see what's inside. Dad will be proud of us."

"I don't know if I can do this," she says as she downs her glass.

"Of course you can." I sound like the parent. An odd excitement creeps over me as I take the key from her hand. This is like getting a little bit of my brother back. I'm touching the footlocker he touched.

I put the key in the lock, turn it, and lift the lid. For some reason, I think of Emma. Somebody should let her know about the funeral, but I don't know about it either. Did Mom and Dad forget?

Bri used to throw his clothes in a drawer when Mom made him clean his room, but now everything is perfectly folded.

I rock back on my knees, holding his clothes in my arms and breathing in a combination of Brian, the scent of jasmine, and the sands of Afghanistan. "Where should I put these?" I ask Mom as I lift out pieces of his Army uniforms.

She sobs, and I know I'm on my own.

I keep pulling out shirts and pants in a desert camouflage print and socks and briefs and undershirts in sandy beige. I find his mess kit and Army gear and an envelope marked *Emma*. Mom might want to read it herself. Helloooo. It might be personal, Mom.

Another envelope is labeled *To My Family*.

"Mom?"

Tears run down her cheeks. I hand her a Kleenex and say, "There's an envelope addressed 'To My Family.' I'm going to open it, okay?"

She nods.

The emblem on the top tells me it's written on Army-issued notepaper. "If you're reading this, I'm either gone or so severely wounded that the Army's sent you my possessions," I read to Mom. She sets down her glass and looks up.

"Frankly, I don't know which would be worse. I don't want to think about it. This is a precautionary measure. Sarge said we all have to do it. It's not like he's going to check it or anything, but I'm lying here in my bunk thinking of you, and I decided I might as well put my thoughts on paper and stick them in my footlocker, just in case.

"You guys know I love you, right?

"Dad, I'm proud to serve, and I can't wait to tell you about the technology we use and the security we have.

"Mom, I love you. Hanging with the guys in this platoon, I know you and Dad raised me right. I wish I'd said I love you more often when I was home.

"Sandee, you take good care of Spike for me, okay? I know you love him as much as I do. You're a cool chick in your own way. If I weren't your brother, I'd tell you you're pretty. Be who you are. Everybody else is taken, just like Mom and Dad kept telling me all through high school.

"The Army changes you. It makes you a team player no matter who you used to be. I'm still figuring out who I am. I know you are too, Sandee, so here's a bit of advice I should have given you before I left home:

Stay away from burnouts.

Pick your battles while you still can.

Don't be afraid of the unknown.

Be a team player.

Pick the right team to play on.

If you pick the wrong one, move on.

"If I don't come home, I'll see all of you on the other side. This is so long—not good-bye."

Mom grabs a handful of Kleenex. I say nothing. There's nothing to say. Bri is gone, and we have no way to get him back.

I'm never going to forget you, Bri. I can't stop talking to him. I sure hope he gets the message even though he's gone.

CHAPTER TWENTY-THREE

HAD SARGE CONVINCED BRI that there was a heaven called The Other Side, or had war opened Bri up to new possibilities?

How can I tell now that he's gone? I can't even hear his voice right now. I keep thinking about the sign for the psychic on Telegraph Avenue.

I Google "trustworthy psychics." I can't find her address there, so I click on "spiritualist psychics." Thirteen pages come up. Is thirteen lucky or unlucky?

There are lots of Yelp listings and lots of opinions. "Trust your intuition," a voice tells me. I have no idea if it's my conscience or Bri. I want it to be Bri, but it's so fast and unexpected. The words are his, but the little voice in my head sounds an awful lot like me.

I pick three psychics who use the word "angel" in their ads, and I call each one. Please be an angel, Bri, I think as the phone rings. No answer. Not even a request to leave a message.

When the next one picks up, a live male voice asks if I'm eighteen; I hang up.

On the last call, a woman talks in a warm voice that makes me want to answer her questions. I tell her my brother died and ask if she can get through to him. She offers to try, but she makes no guarantees. I ask if she's still open from eleven to seven and she says yes. I ask if I need an appointment and she says no. I feel both nervous and fluttery as I hang up and put her address into my cell.

I grab some cash out of an envelope hidden at the bottom of my desk drawer and tell Mom that Diego and I are running an errand for the show. I'm telling the truth. I'll be a better ASM if I'm not obsessing about Bri. It's plausible enough, and it's not like my parents can offer me any better solution.

I stand in front of Diego's house and text, "Going 2 Berkeley 2 see psychic. Come?"

He texts back, "U crazy?"

A minute later, he slips out the front door. "You're not going alone," he says. "For what it's worth, you make other girls look boring."

"You're so sweet. I told my mom we were running an errand for the show."

"Same line I used. I know it's a stretch, but I'm helping you, and that helps the show."

"Great minds think alike." We pass the new condos and turn the corner by the school. Its parking lot is vacant.

We sit together on the empty bus, and I buy tickets for both of us at the BART station. As we pull away on the thin track, which winds through the hills towards Lafayette, Diego takes my hand. A minute later, he removes his earbuds and says, "Sandee, what's up?" even though he already knows.

"I'm glad you're coming with me," I say to distract him.

"What's up?" he asks again.

"Bri's footlocker was in the living room when I got home. Mom and I opened it up, and I read a note to Mom and Dad and me. He said his sergeant made everybody in the platoon write one. At the end of it, he said if we got the note, he'd 'see us the other side.' That doesn't sound like Bri, and it made me curious. I want to know where he is and if he's right about the other side. If he can talk through a psychic, I think he'll tell me, don't you?"

"I dunno."

That's not what I want to hear. I stare out the window. If he doesn't believe me, why did he come?

As we pull into Lafayette, we pass the hill that's jammed full of white crosses. "I wonder how it works," I say more to the smudgy window than Diego.

"The crosses or the psychic?" he asks.

"Both."

"What if this psychic lies?"

I don't have an answer, and I don't want to argue, so I close my eyes. A couple minutes later, he squeezes my hand and says, "So where is this psychic?"

I open my eyes and say, "She has an office on Alcatraz, close to Ashby BART. She said she'd do a reading for $75."

"You know most psychics are phonies, don't you?"

"It's worth the risk." I hope I'm right. He keeps holding my hand, even though I turn away. I can't tell him I'm afraid. My voice will crack. He doesn't get it because Bri isn't his brother. Wasn't. Bri wasn't his brother.

The door to Madame Naomi's office is coated with layer on layer of white paint and it sticks. I can't open it, so Diego and I tug on the latch together until the sticky thing finally budges. I look behind me. No one's watching. Together, we go in.

Thick maroon curtains cover the windows. Forest-green tapers flicker in brass candlesticks on either side of a guest book that sits on a scarred wooden counter. A small sign says, *Sign in please. I'll be with you as soon as possible.*

I sign *Sandee Elizabeth Mason* in the guest book and sit next to Diego on a hard wooden bench that looks like it might have been a pew in a church.

As soon as I sit down, my cell rings. The screen says *Dad.* I show it to Diego, who takes out one of the earbuds and says, "What can he do? You're already here."

So I pick up and say, "Hi, Dad. Are you home?"

Diego rolls his eyes. I've brought up the one subject I most want to avoid. What is wrong with me?

"Where are you and what's this errand that you're running for the show?" Dad asks in a tone that means business.

"I'll be home soon. Thanks for calling, Dad. It means a lot that you care." I push end before he can answer. At exactly that moment, a throaty voice says, "Sandee Elizabeth Mason?" I silence my phone and look up.

A woman in a flowing gold dress smiles at both of us. Her blue-black hair is piled on top of her head, and her dark eyes are lined with kohl.

"I didn't mean to startle you, honey. I'm Madame Naomi. How old are you?"

"I'll be sixteen in a couple of weeks."

"And you?" she asks Diego.

"Sixteen in about six months. What difference does it make?"

"Do your parents know you're here?"

I'm not a good liar, and I don't feel like Bri's anywhere around, but maybe he'll show up, so I nod.

Her piercing green eyes bore into mine as she asks, "Why did you come?"

"My brother died in Afghanistan. I have so many questions for him. Sometimes psychics can reach people on the other side, can't they?" My heart thumps against my ribs as I speak, and I'm afraid I sound naïve.

"If he wants to talk with you, I can be your medium. Do you think he might want to speak with you?"

I nod again. How is this going to work if I can't even talk?

The candle flames quiver intensely, and I wondered if Bri just showed up or it's a breeze.

"And you?" she asks Diego as if nothing happened.

"She's my friend, and I wasn't going to let her come alone. "

She smiles. "I'm proud of both of you for seeking the truth. You've been through a terrible loss, honey. Your brother's name starts with a B, doesn't it?"

Oh. My. God. "How did you know that?"

"I'm a medium."

Spooky—but good, too. Maybe this is exactly where I'm supposed to be. "Do you want me to come in?" Diego asks.

"He might not say the same things if you do," Madame Naomi warns us.

"Okay, but I'm right here if you need me."

"Thank you," I whisper. I follow Madame Naomi as she parts the beads that hang in the doorframe of her inner sanctum.

Midnight-blue curtains cover the walls in the back room. In here, more candles flicker. A statue of the Virgin Mary sits next to a wooden chair with red brocade upholstery. Candles surround the statue.

She points to a small chair where I'm supposed to sit, and says, "You know I have to charge you $75 for this, don't you?"

I hand her three twenties and three fives. She slides them into a brocade bag, and sets it under the table. I hope she isn't conning me.

"I like to begin by tuning in," she says, and I wondered if a voice from the other side comes through like she's a radio station. "There are two people behind you, so stay open, even if your brother doesn't come through."

I turn around to look. "I don't see anyone."

She cuts me off. "Let me concentrate." She lowers her eyes. I stare into the candle flames because I don't know where to look.

"Spirits of the Universe, Sandee Elizabeth Mason is with me. She's looking for her brother, who passed over recently." She pauses. I look around. Nothing's happening.

I'm about to get up and go when she says, "I've got somebody here calling himself Grandpa. He's about six feet tall with gray hair. He passed from a condition in his chest."

"Grandpa Travers?" I ask. "Is your grandson with you? Is Bri okay?"

"Your grandpa wants you to know he's proud of you. He says

you need to help your mother. She isn't ready to accept the loss of her son. He's looking in your face right now, and he says, 'You're so beautiful. You look exactly like your grandma.'"

That's true. I have Grandma's short curvy body and her eyes and her cheekbones. Mom has shown me the pictures of her when she was younger, and we could be twins, but how would Madame Naomi know that we look alike—unless she's actually talking to Grandpa?

Grandma still lives in her old family home on Cape Cod. She hasn't been to California since Grandpa died, so I don't know how this woman could know, unless she's the real thing. "Grandpa, is Bri with you?" I ask, staring at the candles and the statues of Mary instead of Naomi.

If he answers, I can't hear him, but Naomi says, "I think I see your brother, right behind your grandpa. He's about six feet, and a charred, black cloud surrounds him. He says the explosion was over before he knew what happened, and he says, 'Tell Mom and Dad I didn't suffer. I'm proud of you, Sandee. Take care of our family, okay? Take care of yourself, too.'"

I want to believe her. "Do you remember what happened, Bri?"

Her throatiness goes deeper, and she almost sounds like Bri as she says, "We heard a giant explosion. It lifted me up, and then my skin was on fire, and sheets of flames rained down on me. I crashed into something dense and hard. The next thing I knew, I was here."

"Where is 'here'?"

"It's not on Earth's maps, but it's beautiful and safe, and I'll see you when you get here."

"How do I know it's really you, Bri?"

She speaks again without repeating my question. "He says, 'Take care of Spike, and take care of Rob. He's more scared than he'd ever admit.'"

"Scared of what?"

Madame Naomi's throaty voice is lower than ever. "Rob needs a family. So do you. There's a lot you don't understand yet, so be careful."

"What don't I understand? What's it like over there?"

"He's fading now," Naomi says. "He needs a lot of rest and repair. Thank you, Universe, for making Brian and Grandpa Travers available to Sandee." She closes her eyes like she did at the beginning, makes two inward circles with her hands, and looks at me. "The connection is gone."

"Was it really Bri?"

"How else would I have known about Rob—or Spike?"

"I can't imagine, but there's something either unreal or otherworldly about all this, and I don't know which."

"It was a pleasure meeting you, Sandee, and if you have more questions, I hope you'll come back another time."

There's no way she could have gotten both Rob's and Spike's names right without my telling her. She spoke to Bri, and Grandpa Travers was there too.

Back in the waiting room, Diego holds up his phone and says, "We're in deep trouble now."

CHAPTER TWENTY-FOUR

"WHAT DO YOU MEAN, 'We're in trouble'?"

"My mom called," Diego says. We leave Madame Naomi's office and push on the door so that it fits back in the jamb. As we shove against it, Diego says, "She should fix that."

"Do you suppose she keeps it that way so she'll know when somebody's about to break in?"

"Why would a psychic need to know that?"

It's dusk as we walk up Alcatraz towards Ashby BART. A couple of ten-year-old boys whiz by on their scooters. I hear the clank of dinner dishes from a kitchen. All I can see, though, is yellow light coming from a ceiling fixture that's visible above the café curtains.

"My mom called Ms. G to see where I was because I told her we were running an errand for props, remember?"

"Are you kidding me?"

"Ms. G told her I might be with my band. Mom says she can't trust me, and you've got to call and explain why we're here, or she'll pull me out of my band and the show."

"You want me to tell your mom I came to Berkeley to see a psychic? How will that help your credibility?" A man slurping from a small brown bag stumbles past us. "She'll think I've gone over the edge, and I haven't. I heard from Grandpa and Bri."

"Yeah. Right."

"Stop it," I say, thwacking him with my scarf. "Bri talked about Spike and Rob. By name. Madame Naomi didn't know their names."

"You serious?"

"His body's dead, but his spirit must be somewhere. How else could she have gotten those names? I don't know how mediums work, but nobody but Bri would ask me to watch out for Rob or take care of Spike, and how would Madame Naomi know both names if she was faking it?"

"Google?"

"She didn't know who I was before we showed up."

"This is a little spooky."

"I never put it together, but Rob lost his dad, and a few years later, he lost his best friend, and his mom's always working. Bri's right. He is alone. I'll bet that's why he keeps having his Friday night parties. His mom might not even know. She's always at work on Friday nights."

The same two boys whiz past again, one on either side of us, going the opposite way. They skim really close, and Diego takes my hand again.

"So the trip was worth it. I get that, but now you've got to help me. Call my mom." He hands me his cell, which is already ringing.

"Diego?"

"No, Mrs. Rivera. It's Sandee."

"Is Diego all right?"

"Absolutely. He'll be home in about an hour. He didn't want me to come over to Berkeley alone."

She cuts me off. "Are you with his band?"

"No. We came for props. We needed . . . uhhh, things. To make the show more authentic."

"Did you find them?"

"We found exactly what we need, and now we're coming home." I end the call before she can say another word and thrust Diego's cell into his hand. "Quick. What can we get for the show? What does Cord Elam need that would guarantee he's totally in character?" He stares at me like I'm a basket case. "Come on. It's perfect. Prop? Costume piece?"

"I can't believe she bought it."

"Quick! What can we get at the Ashby flea market?"

"Maybe I'm a whittler and I have a fancy knife," he says in a voice so slow and deep that he sounds like Cord Elam.

I stop him. "A knife?"

"Well, we're using the guns." We head into the parking lot that the flea market uses on the weekends. "It's a prop—not a weapon. It might work."

We wander up one aisle and down the next through rugs and clothes and old TVs. Maybe we could get a stage knife, but I don't think it would cut wood. You can't get a stage knife in San Ramos, and that's all that really matters.

"Do you have any stage knives?" I ask the owner of one booth after another. The only one we find looks as bad as I was afraid it would. A salesman bundled up in a suede jacket flips it into the air and says, "It looks fabulous under stage lights."

"Let's get a real knife," Diego says.

"We can't legally bring a knife on campus. Do you think Cord Elam smokes a pipe?"

"So it's okay to smoke on stage?" he shoots back.

"You wouldn't actually smoke it. Does Cord Elam use a trick rope or fiddle with a rabbit's foot?"

"He whittles." He turns to the salesman and asks, "Does this thing cut wood?"

"You can make it look that way." He shows us how to hold his hands so Cord Elam looks like he's whittling. It will work for someone who hangs out in the back of the crowd.

"Let's get a pipe too. Ms. G won't let me smoke it, but we need more than one thing to show Mom."

One of the sellers has at least a dozen old pipes, and Diego tries puffing on one. Holding it, he looks older. I know this isn't what Ms. G meant when she told him to work on his character, but he isn't in drama, so he doesn't know anything about objectives. An actor has to know what his character wants. Right now Cord Elam wants a pipe, and he doesn't care about school rules, so we buy one. We'll worry about the fallout later.

"You're awfully quiet," Diego says as we get on BART to go home.

I'm rerunning what Madame Naomi told me Bri said. Why could he say more to her than he ever did to me? I have more questions than ever now: Are you watching? Can you see the future from there? Can you tell me if the show's going to be good? Am I going to get my driver's license? Bri, am I clairaudient if I can only hear you some of the time?

I found the term clairaudient when I looked at the psychic websites. A clairaudient hears voices.

How am I going to talk about my messages from Bri without sounding crazy? Rob will treat me like a brainless chick, and Nicole and Jenn will roll their eyes. Even Diego has doubts. It doesn't seem real to me either, but I know what happened. Maybe if I e-mail Madame Naomi, she can tell me what to do.

We watch the neighborhood lights through the windows as the train travels to McArthur and then on out into Lafayette and Walnut Creek.

Diego loans me an earbud so we can listen to his music together. I'm glad he came, but I'm even more glad that he believes me as much as he can. How do you prove something when there is no tangible evidence?

CHAPTER TWENTY-FIVE

"CUT," MS. G CALLS after Diego whips out his new knife. "What's in your hand, Cord Elam?"

"A knife. Cord Elam likes to whittle." A couple of seniors groan.

"Maybe he does, but he only whittles in the bunkhouse after work," Ms. G says. The same seniors laugh, and I feel sorry for him. "Diego, you know we can't have a knife on stage. Zero tolerance. It's not negotiable."

"We were afraid you'd say that." He sighs and sits on the steps leading up to Aunt Eller's porch.

"We?"

"Sandee and me. She told me you wouldn't let me use it, but I wanted to try, just in case."

"Sandee was right."

"So how about this?" Diego asks, pulling a pipe out of his other pocket.

"Why is Cord Elam smoking a pipe?" Ms. G asks.

"He likes the odor." He looks at the other actors. No one's laughing this time, and Nicole smiles and nods. "And . . . uh, the tobacco soothes him."

"Go on."

"Ever since his first wife died, he's had a nervous condition that makes it difficult for him to relate to girls, and he thinks a pipe makes him . . . uh, well, uh, more . . . appealing." Diego's voice goes deeper as he speaks.

Nicole leans over and whispers, "You're catching on."

"Way to go, Diego," I shout from the wings.

Tessa stares at me, and Ms. G says, "The cheering squad in the wings is right. Is that you, Sandee?"

My face grows warm. "Uh, yeah. I got carried away."

"It's okay, Sandee. Diego, you're finding Cord Elam's motivations. That's excellent. Try using the pipe in the run-through after the break, and we'll see what happens, okay? No tobacco though. Understood?"

He nods.

"Take ten, everybody."

The actors pull out cell phones and water bottles as they return to the world of homework, tests, and Friday night adventures.

"I can't believe it worked," Diego whispers over the props table.

I double-check to make sure everything is in its proper place. Maybe I'm obsessing about objects, but it's my job. "What worked?"

"She bought our story about the props. We're completely off the hook for our little trip into the afterlife on Saturday."

"Trip into the afterlife?"

"You know what I mean," he says, and a couple of kids standing near us in the darkened wings look over.

My queasy stomach warns me that lying has consequences. Nicole and I both know that even if Diego doesn't. "I wish you'd been in Madame Naomi's back room with me. If you'd heard what she said, you wouldn't call it a trip into the afterlife."

"If it was real to you, Sandee, that's good enough for me, but it'll sound a little flaky to some of the kids around here."

"Whatever."

"Did you hear the cast just now? They love what I made up about the pipe."

"That's great, Diego." I mean it, but it comes out sarcastic.

"You can't stand to have anybody else do something right, can you?"

"How can you say that? We did this together. Are you trying to pick a fight with me so you'll have an excuse to go out with Jenn?"

"Don't be an idiot." He stomps away, and I want to tell him an old man wouldn't stomp.

Instead I yell, "Fine."

"Fine," he yells back. Boys! Six weeks ago he didn't even want to be an actor.

I'm locking the padlock on the props cabinet when I hear Ms. G's footsteps. I think she's there to see what the shouting's about, but she says, "So you took Diego shopping. That's not how I thought you'd help him get in character, but it worked."

"You have to start somewhere," Rob adds because he followed her up here and has to be a part of every conversation. I'm surprised to hear him defending me. "Let's see if the pipe helps him relax and become the character."

"You're starting to think like a director, Rob," Ms. G says and walks away.

Rob puts a hand on my shoulder after she leaves and says, "We techies have to stick together." If that's supposed to be an apology for his attitude back when we picked up the surrey, I accept, but before I can say so, he asks, "Do you still fool around with photography?"

"I mostly use my cell phone, but—"

"Your cell is fine. Think you could take a few shots of the first run-through from backstage?"

"Of course." Standing around watching the props is not the most exciting job in the world. I'm grateful to have more to do. "What are you looking for?"

"Actors in character. Actors getting into character. Dancers stretching. Anything that shows where we are right now. I'm not exactly sure how we're going to use them, but Ms. G wants rehearsal photos. I'll be on book, so Tessa's going to get some shots from the house, and between the two of you, I think we've got it covered."

"I didn't know Tessa took pictures."

"She's got a good eye for composition, which is why Ms. G keeps inviting her to do set decoration, and a camera on her cell, just like you."

"Thanks for giving me the job, Rob. Hey, that rhymes." We both laugh, and I think he winks. Once he's gone, I whisper, "I'm being nicer to Rob, Bri. Did you notice?"

I listen carefully, but I can't hear his answer. Maybe I need to be in a quieter place. Maybe I need lit candles like the ones Madame Naomi used—or maybe he disagrees. How can I tell, if he won't talk to me?

During the run, I shoot actors tipping their cowboy hats and actresses twirling in long skirts with total joy shining on their faces. I shoot girls looking coy and guys winding ropes and tucking prop guns into their holsters. I have a shot of Diego talking to empty space. In the photo, he looks like he's talking to a ghost, but I know he's practicing his lines. It's a good collection of shots, and I hope I got what Rob wants.

At the end of any run, actors and techies sit together, legs swinging from the edge of the stage as we wait for Ms. G's notes. Before I join the actors, I need to put away the props. I turn back to the table and see Jenn standing there, her cheeks flushed from the excitement of the finale. "I need to ask you something, sort of as a representative of Student Council, if that's okay." Her voice trembles. She's never sounded nervous before.

"What's up?"

"I know this must be hard for you, but I'm wondering if you could bring a couple of Bri's trophies or something for a display case that Student Council's putting together. We want to honor our graduates serving in the military, and we get to use the display case in the main hall."

"Sure, Jenn. I can bring you something."

"Something good, okay? Something that shows that he was, like, getting ready to be a hero while he was here."

"Sure," I say again, even though Bri never thought of himself as a hero. I scoop up the last of the props, but she doesn't go away.

As I lock the door to the cabinet, she says, "There's something else. Do you think we could be friends again? I told you I was sorry about what I put on Facebook, but you can't let it go."

"Of course I can," I say, staring at some mud splattered on my Sperry Top-Siders. They were cute when I bought them, but now they look a little ragged. How long since I went to the mall?

"Why are you still ignoring me? It's embarrassing."

Jenn's never cared what I think. Why now? I look at the worry lines on her forehead and say, "We're both just busy with school and rehearsal. I'm not holding a grudge."

"Thank goodness. I was afraid maybe you wanted to get back at me for hanging out with Diego."

I stare at her like Bowen stares at me when I get stuck on a math problem. If she feels guilty, I want to know why. "When you two went to Berkeley, he and I were working on a project for World Cultures. As soon as you called he said, 'I gotta go, Jenn. Sandee needs me,' and ran out the door."

"We were just looking for props."

"Right. A pipe and a rubber knife. In Berkeley. I watched the two of you heading for the BART bus. Where did you really go?"

"To Berkeley."

"I hate it when nobody trusts me." Jenn looks as upset as I felt after I auditioned.

"Ms. G asked me to try to help Diego with his character," I say in my most soothing voice.

"Yeah, but why did he jump when you called?"

"Who knows? I'll bring you some of Bri's things, I promise, and just so you know you can trust me, I'll show you some photos I got during the run-through."

"Why were you taking photos?"

"Rob asked me to." I pull them up on my phone. She looks totally confused. I almost ask her why, but a little voice in my head says, "She's not used to seeing you in charge."

"What are you grinning at?" she asks.

If I really wanted to push her over the edge, I'd tell her I visited a medium in Berkeley, and she told me things only Bri could have said, and now Bri's just sent me another message. At least, I think it's from Bri.

CHAPTER TWENTY-SIX

THE NEXT MORNING, MISS Bowen collects our math homework. I see age spots across the knuckles on her left hand. I never noticed them before. Bri won't ever get . . . I have to stop this. Bri's gone. He wouldn't want me thinking about him every second, would he?

An aide comes in with a note, and everybody stares as she hands it to Miss Bowen, who peers at it through her half-glasses and says, "Sandee, the principal needs to see you."

I hear the usual groans, giggles, and "Busteds" as I stuff my algebra book into my backpack.

Once I'm outside, though, I pump my fist and say, "All right!" I haven't done anything wrong, and Dr. Henderson's just gotten me out of Bowen's weekly quiz. Diego will take it third period, tell me what's on it, and I'll make it up at lunch. Outside the principal's office Mom and Dad sit on matching chairs. It looks like Mom's been crying again, and my heart thumps in my chest.

"What's up?" I ask at the same moment the principal's secretary says, "Dr. Henderson will see you now." I follow my parents into his office, feeling like a little child instead of the confident young woman I was when Jenn talked to me last night.

"We're all so sorry about Brian," Dr. Henderson says as we settle on the blue chairs in front of his cluttered desk. "How are you adjusting?"

I stare at the cream-green wall behind Dr. Henderson's desk. Four posters with *Courage, Attitude, Integrity,* and *Focus* in bold letters hang there. I know they're supposed to inspire a better attitude, but a better attitude won't bring Bri back. I get so tired of feeling less than Bri because I didn't die.

"We'd like to find a way to honor him at the same time we educate our students about war," Dr. Henderson says. He's staring at me, not Mom and Dad. "Student Council is putting together a display case honoring our graduates serving in the military, and I thought we might call everyone's attention to the individuals involved with an assembly."

"What would you want us to do?" Dad asks.

"We'd like you to share a video or slideshow about your son. Would that be possible?"

Mom's eyes fill as she looks at Dad. Dr. Henderson says, "Sandee's taking one of our computer classes, and I'm sure she knows how to put a PowerPoint together if you have some scrapbooks she can work from."

"We have scrapbooks," Dad says. Mom has a whole CD of photos, not to mention a ton of albums. She took photos at every birthday party, track meet, and awards ceremony until Bri went away.

"It might give you some closure to work on it together," Dr. Henderson suggests.

Mom and Dad don't want closure. They want Bri back.

"We're going to ask a couple of other families to participate as well. One has a daughter with a traumatic brain injury and one has a father on active duty."

When he says a daughter with a traumatic brain injury, I think of Tessa, though there are probably others who fit that description. She can throw a PowerPoint together in five minutes, and her mom speaks all the time. My stomach knots, probably because I don't want to compete with Tessa or anyone else. Then I hate that I even had that thought. Nobody said this was a competition. I'm a mess, and I don't know how to fix it. How do I get past the fact that Bri doesn't even have to be on the planet to be the family hero? I know it's a crappy way to feel, but I'm not responsible for my feelings. They pop up out of nowhere.

"There's one other thing we'd like to include. We'd like one of you to talk about Brian," Dr. Henderson says. He's staring at me again. "Tell us what he was like before he got to high school. Tell us why he joined the Army and what he hoped to do when he got out. Tell us something we don't already know about him. Sandee, would you be willing to speak?"

"Me?" I'd be talking about Bri, but I'd be the one in front of the whole school. I'd be the one everybody was looking at.

"Yes, Sandee. You're his sister. The kids will relate to you more than they would to your parents." He turns to them and adds, "Of course, I'm sure she'll get your input."

"I'd be happy to do it," I say in a voice that's softer than I expected. "I'll tell about Little League and Boy Scouts and his Science Club projects and track. Maybe I could interview some of the kids who remember him from Student Council. Maybe even a teacher or two."

Dr. Henderson beams. "That's the spirit, Sandee, and of course we want your parents at the assembly. Other parents will be there too."

Rob knew Bri better than anybody, I think at the same moment Dr. Henderson asks, "Do you have the time to do this with your schoolwork and the play, Sandee?"

"Of course. When's the assembly?"

"We're going to hold it the Wednesday after next at 10 a.m. That should give you plenty of time.

"That's right before—"

He holds up a hand to stop me. "I know it's the day before *Oklahoma!* opens, but we've checked with Ms. Gittinger, and she has no problem with our doing it in front of a closed curtain even though your sets will be up. Now, can you be ready?"

"Absolutely." I have seventeen days to put something spectacular together. That's over half a month.

Dr. Henderson gives me a pass and sends me back to class.

"Bri, are you good with this?" I ask as soon as I'm alone in the hall. I don't hear an answer, but for a minute, I think I see him standing at the far end of the hall in front of the heavy green breakaway doors, nodding yes.

Some guy behind me calls, "Sandee?" I turn and see Diego at his locker. "How was the quiz?" he asks.

I explain why I missed it and ask him to meet me at the end of fourth so he can tell me what's on it.

"I'll try," he promises, and slams his locker door.

That's all any of us can do. Bri is gone and so is the figure at the end of the corridor. Sometimes I'm afraid my imagination is taking my mind on a roller coaster ride.

I listen to the emptiness in the hall as I head for my locker. It's so quiet I hear a bird chirping in one of the walnut trees. If I can stall for seven minutes, math class will be over.

At lunch, I go to Bowen's classroom for the makeup test. It's not the one Diego described after fourth period. It's harder. I do the best I can, but seriously, doesn't that woman have anything better to do than make up tests? I almost feel sorry for her. She has no family, and her students hate her. I'd say math doesn't run in our family, but Dad's really good at it, so the problem has to be her.

Once I finish the stupid quiz, I text Rob and tell him I need to talk about Bri.

He doesn't respond, and when I walk in to rehearsal that afternoon, he's busy giving notes to actors who missed lines. I offer to help, but he blows me off. While I hand the actors the props they need, I try to imagine myself in front of the school speaking about Bri.

Three of the supporting actors sit on the floor doing homework, and I take a couple of shots of them with my cell. I also get shots of an actor in a cowboy hat and a holster texting. It looks like someone from the wrong century has popped up in the Old West. Ms. Marron says when that happens it's an anachronism. I don't suppose a person who gets to heaven too early could be considered an anachronism. More like a horrid mistake.

"Can I talk to you?" I ask Rob again once rehearsal ends and we are leaving the theater.

"Are your props secured?"

"Check them yourself if you need to."

"Sandee, don't get defensive. I'm doing my job."

Is part of your job mistrusting everyone? Instead of saying it out loud, I focus on Bri's message, and the assembly, and say, "I need to talk to you about Bri." He keeps walking, so I follow him out the door past the music building to the parking lot where his Honda waits for him in the student section.

"What do you want to ask me about Bri?" Rob finally says.

"What are your best memories of him?"

He turns and glares in a way that makes me shiver.

"So, what do you remember?" I ask, even though his eyes are shooting daggers at me.

"He's gone, Sandee. What difference does it make?"

When I try to tell him about the assembly, the words won't come out.

Instead I say, "Don't you like remembering?"

"It won't change anything." He unlocks the door and climbs in. "We used to have each other's backs, but he had to go off to try and save the world. Now he's dead, and I'm left behind. Remembering him won't change that."

"I'm sorry. I didn't mean to upset you. Can you drive me home?"

He nods, so I open the passenger door while he slides a CD labeled Mellow Mix into the right slot on his dashboard. "You didn't upset me," he mumbles as he hits Play. He lies. I understand why, but today I need the truth.

He starts the engine, and I don't ask if I can drive. After a minute, he lowers the volume on the CD and says, "He was older. He was smart. He came from a whole family complete with a pesky little sister."

"Yeah yeah," I say when I hear the little sister crack. "What's the best thing you ever did on a Saturday?"

"Are you making a documentary?" I'm pretty sure he's joking, but his question makes it easier to explain about the assembly and the fact that Dr. Henderson wants me to talk about Bri.

He doesn't go off in a rage. Instead he says, "So you're looking for answers suitable for school, right?"

"Duh," I say as he swings around the corner faster than I would. "Maybe I should ask what's the best thing you ever did that wasn't suitable for school."

"You're better off not knowing some things." He pulls into the gas station, puts on the brake, and turns off the engine. "Can I borrow sixty?"

"Are you kidding? I don't have that kind of money."

"Loan me thirty, and I'll let you drive."

I pull out a twenty. He snatches it from my hand and goes inside to pay the cashier.

I move into the driver's seat, and when he comes back, he says, "What are you doing there?"

"I'll drive and you answer my questions, okay?"

"Out." He stands beside the door, waiting.

"What is your problem?"

"Fill it and maybe you can drive," he says instead of answering my question. It's better than sitting around, which is what he does, while the gas pump races up to $20.

"You owe me," I say when I get back in. The driver's seat is taken and he won't move. "Remember when you and Bri hung out at our house every Saturday?"

He nods.

"You were in ninth grade and Bri was in tenth, right?"

He nods again.

"Why were you there every Saturday?"

"Nobody yelled at your house, and you were three years younger than Bri, so we could push you around."

"Excuse me?"

"Seventh-grade girls with flat chests are always pests to ninth and tenth-grade boys. Now that you've filled out, you're a whole lot sexier."

I want to ask if he really thinks I'm sexy, but instead I ask, "Did it bother Bri that you were younger?"

We listen to the asthmatic hum of his motor until he says, "I don't remember. He tried to be perfect, you know. Maybe I gave him the courage to defy his dad." A minute later he asks, "Why is Henderson making you do this?"

"He thought the kids would relate better to me than to my parents."

He snorts. "Shows how much he knows. Kids don't relate to dweebs."

"What are you talking about? I'm no dweeb. A minute ago you called me sexy."

He laughs and says, "I'll bet he did it cuz you're foxier than your mom." My cheeks are on fire, but we both pretend they aren't.

"What does Rob Cooper want the world to know about Brian Mason?"

"He was a good guy. He gave his life for his country, and now he can't find a cure for cancer or be a politician or cover for you when you come home late from a hot date."

"I can use most of that. Thanks."

"Use all of it—or are you too young for hot dates?"

My cheeks feel like fire. His music pounds inside my skull. "Did Bri ever let you drive his car before you had your license?"

"Why are you changing the subject?"

"Why aren't you answering my questions?"

"Because this is more fun."

I roll my eyes.

"Tell you what. Send me five questions once you get inside, and if I don't text you answers tonight, I'll give them to you tomorrow." Then he reaches across the console, draws me to him, and kisses me on the lips. I start to pull away, but a second later I lean in. The kiss is long and luxurious. My heart thunders against my ribs.

My head is still in that kiss as I write my questions:

What do you miss most about Bri?

What's your favorite story about Bri?

What did you think when you heard he was going into the Army?

What do you think Bri would want us to know about him?

Do you really think Bri could have cured cancer?

I text them to Rob, and say, "Tell me tomorrow, k?" Then I text the same questions to Diego, Dad, and Mom and add, "I need material for the assembly." After I click send, I look around. I'm completely alone, so I say, "Are you watching me, Bri? I'm going to do this right and make you proud."

I hear the heater hum. I swivel in my chair, and it squeaks. If Bri answers, I can't hear his words. Maybe he's watching somebody else's life at this moment—or maybe when you're dead, you're gone.

I fear that, but I don't believe it. I've heard his voice before. I'll hear it again.

CHAPTER TWENTY-SEVEN

AN HOUR AFTER I send my texts, I sneak into Bri's room. I run my hand over the little raised squares on the outside of his footlocker. Dad asked me to stay away from it, but he wouldn't give me a reason, and I already looked once, so I unfasten the hasps, and try to lift the lid. It won't come up because Dad put Bri's padlock back on. How stupid! What in the world are they trying to hide? Bri's dead. Nothing can hurt him anymore. I don't get this. Locking me out never works.

I'm on my way to see if I have a key that will fit when I see the Army envelope with Emma's name in Bri's cursive. It's sitting on the edge of his dresser. Why would Mom and Dad leave it there instead of forwarding it?

Bri asked Mom and Dad to take care of Emma on the day he left for boot camp. He said she'd be their daughter as soon as he got back. Then they kissed each other, and Emma glowed as she held up her left hand and showed us her promise ring.

Now, I run my fingers around the edge of the envelope, wondering if I should hand-deliver it. UC Berkeley is only a BART ride away. Maybe she'll give me a great quote for my speech about Bri.

I slide the note into my backpack and head for the door. Maybe Mom and Dad will decide I'm growing up if I deliver it without being asked. A BART bus stops in front of San Ramos High in sixteen minutes. I pull on my fleece jacket. I have to hurry.

When I climb on board, I hear the pushing and shoving of kids even before I see three middle school boys acting like children. They sit on the opposite side of the aisle from two girls with more makeup than the hookers in downtown Oakland. They think they're cool. They're wrong.

I say, "You're too loud," in my best ASM voice. They laugh. I glare, and they laugh harder, but as soon as I turn my back, they quiet down. Maybe Dr. Henderson is right. Maybe the kids at school will listen to me.

Mom and Dad are both supposed to be home by six, so I text them, "Running an errand. Might be late." That's the absolute truth, and if they want to ask me where I went, I'll tell them.

I change trains at MacArthur, and when we stop at Ashby, I stare through the window down the street to Madame Naomi's office. Were Diego and I here less than a week ago?

I want to read Bri's note to Emma, but it's sealed. Besides, it might be a final letter like he wrote to us, and Emma will share it if she wants to. After all, she's practically family.

The sun sends long shadows down Addison Street as I emerge from the Downtown Berkeley Station. A musician sits on the concrete sidewalk, strumming his guitar. Men in suits and women in heels hurry past his open guitar case. Three bills sit all alone, and when I look in, I realize they're ones. I reach in my pocket and drop another dollar in. He needs it more than I do.

I zip up my hoodie as I cross Shattuck and head for Putnam Hall, where Emma lives on the fifth floor with three other freshmen girls. Students hurry past me like they're late for class or work or the library or dinner. I haven't thought about food since lunch, and I haven't bought M&Ms for three days. Not even a small package. I know there are some in the bottom of my backpack, but right now, I'm not even interested.

I don't know when the craving for candy stopped. I hope it's not just a reaction to the stress that came with Bri's footlocker. I used to think nothing could be worse than not knowing what happened to him, but now I'm not so sure. There's a hollow place in my stomach, and food can't fill it.

I walk into Putnam Hall behind a young woman with tight jeans and a key card. Nobody notices, so no one questions me. I find the stairs, climb to the third floor, and knock on #323, which is Emma's door.

I hear a gasp, a giggle, and the sounds of people scurrying around. Then Emma says, "I'll be right there," in a breathy voice.

She opens the door, and her blonde hair is streaked with navy-blue highlights. She wears skinny jeans, a dark-blue UC Berkeley sweatshirt, and flip-flops. "What happened to your hair?" I ask.

Emma reaches for her glasses before she says, "Sandee? Is that you?"

"Yes. I sent you a text from BART. Didn't you get it?"

"Uhhh, no. I've been really busy."

Hairy feet step into loafers on the far side of a folding screen. Emma says, "I'm sorry, Sandee. I wasn't expecting you. My friend Daniel is here. You want to come in?"

I step inside and look at the white walls covered with bookshelves and posters and colorful storage cubes. Bri will never have a dorm room.

"Come on in. We're just studying."

"Hey, Sandee," Daniel says as he comes out from behind the screen. He wears a rumpled plaid shirt and jeans that need washing. "Are you Emma's little sister?"

"I'm her boyfriend's sister," I say before I remember that's not what you say if the boyfriend's dead. What should I say? Her deceased boyfriend's sister? That sounds awful.

"You didn't tell me you have a boyfriend," Daniel says.

Emma's blue streaks wag as she shakes her head. "He was my high school sweetie. He went into the Army, and we agreed to see other people." Then she says, "Maybe he didn't tell you that, Sandee, but—"

I take a step back and hold up my hand to stop her. "That doesn't sound like Bri."

"Big brothers don't always tell their little sisters everything. You should know that much by now. So, what are you doing here?"

I look around. "Could we . . . maybe talk alone?"

"Why don't you go get us a couple of cups of coffee, Daniel?" He reaches for his wallet, but she hands him a ten-dollar bill.

He pockets it, grabs his jacket, and says, "Good plan."

"Try Sonoma. The coffee's good and the lines are short." He glares. "Fine. Go to Starbucks, like always, but Sonoma's closer and their coffee's local."

"Women."

We ignore him as he slams the door. "So what's up, Sandee? Why are you here?"

My heart crashes into my ribs. I can hardly breathe. "Did my dad call you about Bri?"

"I know he's been missing for over eight months."

I hand her the envelope with Bri's writing on it.

"He's gone, isn't he?" she asks before she even opens it. She can't call him dead either. She puts her arms around me and says, "I'm sorry, honey. This must be so hard for you. I'm surprised your dad asked you to deliver this."

I can't tell her he doesn't know I'm here. Instead, I stare at her hands, which shake as she struggles to open the envelope. I watch her face as she reads. I watch her eyes stop moving. She doesn't look up.

"I'm sorry, Emma. The note's been sitting on his dresser. I thought someone should bring it to you."

She squirms and then says, "I know what you think about Daniel, but he understands math and statistics and all that stuff, and I need his help. We're just friends, like you and . . . um, Diego?"

I can't see Diego and me having an argument about where to buy coffee, but I don't say so. Besides, Diego's more than a friend, now, and I'm afraid that Daniel is more than a friend to Emma.

She pats my arm, and says, "I'm sorry he's gone and sorry you had to bring this to me. He said his dad would do it, and he asked me to be strong for him and tell his dad I still loved him, even if I'd moved on."

"Moved on?" I stare at the titanium cover of her closed iBook. Why is it closed and sitting on the desk if they were studying?

"Don't misunderstand. Bri and I loved each other, but he stopped e-mailing after he'd been there a few weeks, so I figured he found someone else."

I glance around her colorful dorm room. Clothes in other girl's sizes and enough books to start a library fill the space. A poster of Justin Bieber hangs on one wall and a *Go Green* poster hangs next to it. Is either one Emma's?

"He went missing after eleven weeks. I know my dad called you."

"Yes, he did."

"So?"

"Being here is wonderful, and the more I thought about him being in Afghanistan instead of in college, the less I understood him."

"Serving your country is an honorable thing to do." I can't believe I'm quoting Dad.

"So is getting an education."

Why is she so defensive? "I'm glad he doesn't know you broke up with him."

"I didn't."

"Of course you did. You just didn't have the courage to tell him." She gasps.

"I'm sorry, Emma. That came out all wrong."

"It's okay. He's your brother—*was* your brother—and there are things you don't understand yet. When will the funeral be?"

"I don't know, but if you want to come and be his girlfriend one last time, it would mean a lot to the people who still think of you two as a couple."

"I'm so sorry this happened."

I can't tell if she even means it. I square my shoulders, like an Army specialist, and say, "You do what you think is right. We'll make excuses if you don't show up." I take a final look at her dorm room as I head for the door.

"When you get older, you'll understand."

I doubt it. My stomach quakes, and M&Ms won't fix it. I meet Daniel on the stairs. He carries three cups of coffee in one of those egg-crate containers and a bag of something that smells deliciously sweet. "Hey, Sandee. Don't go yet. I got a cup for you, too."

"Keep it." Hard to believe I can sound that fierce. I'm not even mad. I'm hurt. "It's not your fault," I add as I rush down the stairs.

"What's up?"

"Ask your stupid girlfriend." My eyes fill with tears.

Outside, the sun's gone down and so has the temperature. Most of the people I pass are in jeans and jackets, but a few girls in dresses and heels are out on dates in the middle of the week. Have any of these girls cheated on a boyfriend in Afghanistan or Iraq or Syria? How common is this agreement to date other people?

Early stars twinkle overhead. Lamplight shines out through some of the windows. I can see why Emma thinks it's exciting here, but she shouldn't judge Bri's decision. Was he too ashamed to tell us they broke up—or did he even know when he died? Sometimes I think I should be an investigative journalist instead of a drama geek.

"Sandee, wait up," a deep voice calls through the crowd.

"Bri?" The word catches in my throat. It isn't Bri's voice, though, and I know it. Daniel is trying to catch up with me.

"Let me walk you to BART."

I walk faster. So does he. "I know it's old fashioned, but Emma says Bri would want her to make sure somebody walked you to BART."

"Why would she care what Bri wants?"

"Slow down. Emma cares about many things and many people." I say nothing. I can't. It hurts too much that she's moved on. "I know how disturbing this must be."

My throat swells. "That doesn't mean she has any right to cheat on him."

"We're friends, Sandee. She hasn't heard from Bri in months, and she's getting on with her life."

"Bri's been MIA, so how could he write?" I say, in case she forgot to tell him.

"Right now she's concerned about you, and I think she has more to say than you're willing to hear."

We're at the entrance to the station. "Bye," I say without looking back at him.

"Are you okay?" he calls down the stairs.

"I bounce back better than most kids," I say, even though it's a lie. Some of us just pretend we're tough and resilient. "Thanks for coming after me, but I can take care of myself."

"You don't have to do this alone."

I wave a hand as I go down the stairs. I blink hard to hold back my tears.

Does Bri have a clue that Emma and Daniel are a couple? Who broke up with whom?

"I'm sorry, Bri," I whisper as I put my ticket into the turnstile. Maybe he says, "Me too," but I don't think so. It's hard to be sure with all the people rushing past and talking on their cells as if this is an ordinary Tuesday evening.

CHAPTER TWENTY-EIGHT

AS SOON AS THE BART train is no longer underground, I pull out my cell and call Nicole. I know she broke up with Rob, and I hope she can help me understand Emma and Bri. Her phone rings three times before I hear, "This is Nicole. I'm not here, but I *really* want to talk to you. Leave a message, okay?"

"It's Sandee. I have a question about you and Rob, but you're not there and . . . and. . . " I can't speak, so I hit end. What is the matter with me? If I can't even leave a message, how am I going to speak about Bri in front of the whole student body?

I stare out the window at the yellow light spilling out from the kitchens and living rooms of the vintage houses in Oakland. I see hanging plants and overstuffed bookshelves inside one apartment, but no movement except a cat on a windowsill twitching its tail. Then there's a darkened room with a flat screen so big that I can read *Crisp 4*, written in green and gold on the back of a ball player's shirt. A minute later, I see the shadows of two people clutching each other. Hasn't anyone told them how unprivate their sofa is whenever BART rolls by?

I want to call Bri and tell him about Emma and Daniel. Get a grip. You can't call heaven—if there is such a place, though I don't know where else a soldier who died for his country would go. I'd call Diego, but how can I explain what I don't understand?

I get off at the MacArthur Station to wait for the next Bay Point train. The platform is full of UC Berkeley students reading and texting. I put my backpack between my feet, dig out my phone and click on the pictures of rehearsal. Sitting here, away from school, I cannot believe how good Diego looks or how animated most of the actors are. No wonder we're one of the best drama departments in the state.

I'm at the end of the pictures when I hear, "Hey, Sandee, what are you doing here?"

I practically jump out of my skin. Tessa's the last person I expect to see here on the McArthur platform.

"I didn't mean to scare you. I spoke at a support meeting over at Harmony Church."

"Wow. Do you go all over?"

"Beats sitting at home or in Kayla's room worrying." We both eye the college kids. Bri won't ever be a college student, and we don't know yet about Kayla. Berkeley might be a bit of a stretch unless she recovers fully.

"Thinking about going to Berkeley next year?" I finally ask to break the silence.

"Maybe. I applied to a lot of places." She looks away, and I wonder what she isn't telling me.

"Tell me about the meeting."

"Same format. Same stories. Different faces. I told them about my sister and that I'd decided I liked not knowing ever since you heard about your brother."

"You mentioned me?"

"Not by name." We both look around at all the people on the platform with normal lives and siblings safe at home. Then she says, "Do you feel different now that you know?"

"Sometimes I feel like I'm losing my mind a little." I've never said those words out loud before, but after seeing Emma, I have to say them to someone. Besides, I trust Tessa. Her question makes me feel wise. "Don't tell anybody, okay?"

"Grief does strange things. Did your parents send you to a shrink?"

"Once. I'm not going back."

"Why?"

I don't want to talk about me anymore, so I say, "We haven't seen you at rehearsal. Is your work all done?"

She takes the hint. "Until we move out of the rehearsal room and into the auditorium."

"What else did you tell those people tonight? I'd like to hear your story." The whir of the train wheels against the track almost drowns out my words.

We board it and sit opposite a map of the four BART lines before she says, "Well, you already know about my sister, and I'm still in high school because I missed so much of my fifth grade year that I had to do it over."

"You missed it?"

She laughs until I start laughing too, even though I don't know why. "I guess I've done a better job of hiding the accident than I thought."

"What accident?"

"When I was ten, my dad was driving me to soccer practice one Saturday. We were on 680 when he got a call on his cell, and then I heard a huge crash and we were upside down. I screamed but nothing came out. The next thing I knew, I woke up in a dark room, and I heard Mom say, 'Her eyes are open. Get a nurse.'"

"OMG! Were you in a coma? What happened?"

"You know how this ends because I'm still here, right?"

I nod.

"I went back to sleep, and when I woke up, Mom was still there. She asked, 'Do you know where you are?' I tried to answer, but nothing came out, so she said, 'Can you blink your eyes?' and when I couldn't she said, 'Can you squeeze my hand?'"

Another train whooshes past us going the opposite direction, and I think how easy it is for everything to be reversed without any warning.

"I don't have the words to ask what's wrong, so I draw Dad driving me to soccer practice with a big question mark next to it, and that's when Mom tells me there's been an accident. I point to Dad and the question mark again, and her eyes fill with tears. I draw a picture of clouds with a question mark, and Mom says, 'Yes, he's in heaven. I'm sure he's watching over us. He'll be with you forever.'"

"Then your sister comes home with a TBI? You and your mom must feel cursed."

Tessa shakes her head. "We're grateful she's alive."

She stares out the window as we pulled into Rockridge. Three boys with backpacks and big voices get off, and a gray-haired man in tweed gets on. We're pulling out before I ask, "Do you ever dream about your dad?"

She smiles a slow, broad grin. "Sometimes I dream that Kayla and I are little and we're all eating dinner together and he won't let us eat dessert because we haven't eaten our veggies, and I used to dream about the day he gave Kayla a catcher's mitt. Silly stuff."

"Real stuff. I only dream about fireworks in the desert."

"When I was thirteen, I started talking to Dad, even though he isn't here anymore. Does that sound weird?"

I shake my head. My heart flutters a little. Maybe I'm not as alone as I thought.

"It's like I'm asking a hidden camera for a second opinion. Does that make sense?" she asks.

"Absolutely. Now." She waits. Again. "It makes sense because I talk to Bri, and sometimes I hear him encouraging me." She doesn't say a word. "Like, right before auditions, he said, 'Go for it, Sandee,' and in the weeks before, I'd hear him say, 'It's going to be all right.'"

"If you're really hearing his voice, you might have a genuine psychic talent. You could be clairaudient."

"So a human being can hear the voice of spirits?" I already know the answer. My heart thunders in my ears of all places. Maybe she's giving me a genuine explanation. Even after seeing Madame Naomi,

I'm not convinced the voice is his, but Tessa's realistic and practical, and she doesn't think it's freaky for me to hear him in my head.

"Have you ever told anyone?"

"Only Diego. He went with me when I came over here to see a psychic. Don't tell anybody, okay?"

"A psychic?"

"Madame Naomi. She told me Bri talked about Spike and Rob, and if she knew both those names, she must have been channeling something real."

Tessa tilts her head and nods slowly, like she's taking it all in.

"How do I know I'm not manufacturing his voice in my head when I'm not with her? And why couldn't I hear him in her office?"

"Maybe Bri's trying to get through to the family, and this is as close as he could come. Do you have any psychic relatives?"

"Not that I know of. What about you?"

She shakes her head.

"Did you discover you could draw because of the accident?" I ask as we pull into the Lafayette Station.

"I suppose. I know I got better and better when I couldn't talk for a year." She stands up and says, "I left the car here."

"Why?"

"My mom's got late clients, and I'm supposed to pick her up after the last one. See you at school." A bunch of commuters push their way off the car. Their massive movement swallows her up.

I stare at the white crosses opposite the BART station, standing straight up against the dark hillside. The white paint glows in the light of the passing cars. Some have Jewish stars or Muslim crescents on them, and they keep getting denser every month. I think we should put up a cross for Bri, but Mom and Dad can't even plan a funeral. Or maybe they won't do that until the body . . . the body parts . . . get here.

I hear "The doors are closing," over and over, but nothing happens. A more accurate statement would be "The doors are trying to close." They start and stop, start and stop, and they remind me of the way

I stop eating M&Ms and then start up again. Today, though, I don't want candy. I'd rather figure out what happened with Emma and Bri and whether Daniel's the reason they broke up, so I try Nicole's cell again. "What's up, Sandee? Are you calling for Ms. G again? Because I've been at every rehearsal."

"Chill. I'm not the rehearsal police. I'm calling 'cause you said I could. Are you at home?"

"Of course. I'm doing my homework and watching my little brothers. What's the noise in the background?"

"The BART doors won't close. I'm coming back from Berkeley."

"What were you doing over there?"

"I went to see Bri's girlfriend." There. It was out.

I explain about the notes in Bri's footlocker, one for me and one for my parents, and a third one for Emma that never got further than Bri's dresser. I tell her about Daniel putting on his shoes and Emma telling me they were studying.

Then I say, "You're closer to college kids than I am. Do you think they're just study partners?"

"I don't know. I wasn't there. Is that what you really called to ask?"

"Partly. Emma says she and Bri agreed to see other people. Is that what happened when you broke up with Rob?"

"We broke up because I was sober and he was still drinking. I care about Rob, but my sobriety comes first."

"So maybe Emma cares about Bri but he's too far away and her education comes first?"

"Maybe," Nicole says in a voice that tells me she doesn't believe it for a second.

Bri's gone. Emma can't hurt him if he's not here, but seeing her with Daniel hurt me. "So why am I obsessing about this?" I ask. She's the expert on obsessions.

"Different people cope in different ways, Sandee. It's certainly better than drowning your sorrows in M&Ms. Do you want Rob and me to come up to BART and pick you up?"

"Wait a minute. I thought you two broke up."

"We did, and I'd pick you up myself, but I don't have my license back."

"I can take the bus. Besides, the train is stuck in Lafayette, and I don't know when I'll get there," I say and click end. I'm tired of talking. Instead, I stare at the crosses. They haven't changed.

I look at all the commuters reading newspapers and Kindles, and finally I get out my English book and open my tattered copy of *Lord of the Flies,* which is our assigned reading for English. I turn page after page, absorbed by a very different war between two groups of boys stranded on an unmarked island during World War II. I've finished my chapters for tonight and started tomorrow night's reading before the train operator announces that the doors will be closing in one minute. Finally, she's right.

In Walnut Creek, I get off with a bunch of commuters and go down the stairs. On the other side of the faded plastic turnstile I see Rob waving at me.

Some twenty-somethings with killer stilettos and huge gestures push past me. I can smell liquor on them, and I'm glad they rode BART instead of driving.

"I'll drive you home," Rob calls across the turnstile. He's slurring his words and sounds as drunk as those girls act.

CHAPTER TWENTY-NINE

"NICOLE SAYS YOU NEED a ride," Rob blurts out as I come through the turnstile. "Whatcha doin' up here anyway?"

I wave my hand in front of my nose. "How many beers have you had?"

"Here I am trying to play Sir Galahad, and you ask if I've been drinking."

"You reek."

"I'm offended." He spurts as he says "offended," and his body teeters.

"How many?"

"Get in the car, little one."

"No way. You're not getting in it either." I reach for his keys, and he yanks them away and dangles them high out of my reach. "Give them to me, Rob. You can't drive like that."

"How do you think I got here?"

I try to pull his arm down, but he says, "Cut that out. People are staring." He's right. A security guard in a BART uniform is glaring at us.

"You're going to get us in trouble," I say through gritted teeth. I reach for the keys, and he stumbles backwards into the ticket machine. He shakes his head and looks puzzled. He's trying to stand up straight, but it's too late. The guard comes over, grabs Rob's right arm, and steps between us. "Is there a problem here?" he asks.

"He's not driving me home. He shouldn't be driving anyone anywhere." Rob looks like he's choking. Two seconds later, he throws up on the guard's shoes. He grabs his mouth and turns away, but it's too late, and he knows it.

"That's disgusting," the man says as a second BART security guard rushes over with a handful of paper towels.

"How much have you had to drink tonight, son?" the second guard asks.

"I'm not your son. I'm not any man's son." The first guard is still wiping vomit off his shoes when the second one grabs Rob and pins him against one of the cement walls near the exit gate. Then he turns to me and says, "What is this boy talking about?"

"Shut up, Sandee," Rob says in a broken voice. He struggles for a few seconds before he pulls himself together and says, "I'm fine. I lost my balance. I don't need your help."

The second security guard, whose badge says Ho, shakes his head. "I need to see your driver's license, young man."

Rob's hands tremble as he opens his wallet and tries to extract his license.

He drops it, and I reach for it, but Mr. Ho puts a hand on my shoulder and shoves me back. "You have problems of your own, missy."

"I don't want him to drive drunk."

"So you create a public brawl?" the first guard asks. I'd be pissed too if someone had thrown up on my shoes, but he's picking on the wrong person.

The drunk bimbos in heels giggle as they wait for their taxi.

"Everybody's overreacting," I say to the girls, the guards, and anybody else within earshot.

"I've got this, Bradley," Mr. Ho says. "They're just a couple of kids."

Bradley shakes his head. His recently dried shoes squeak a little as he returns to his booth.

Ho keeps one hand on Rob's arm and pushes the button on his walkie-talkie with the other. "We've got a couple of kids fighting by the bus stop here at Walnut Creek BART."

"We aren't fighting. We were arguing, and we aren't doing anything illegal." I hope he can't hear my heart pounding into my ribs.

"We think one of them's been drinking, and his license says he's only seventeen."

"Did you see him drive in?" *Where did that come from? Why am I defending Rob all of a sudden?*

Mr. Ho lets Rob's arm go. As soon as he's free, Rob sneaks his license into his jacket pocket. Nobody notices but me because a Walnut Creek police car drives up with its lights blazing. A large woman opens the passenger door and bellows, "What's going on?" She tucks a stray clump of hair back into her bun and straightens her gun belt.

Ho says, "Smell his breath, Bartlett."

"Whew! What's up with the girl?"

"She's sticking her nose in where it don't belong. The two of them are quite a pair."

Officer Bartlett gets in my face and says, "You want to go to juvenile hall for obstruction of justice?" She dangles a pair of handcuffs in front of me.

"No. I'm sorry." My voice trembles. "We're both sorry. We don't want any trouble."

"You should have thought of that before you made such a ruckus," Officer Bartlett says.

"Please don't arrest us." I shiver in the chilly March air. "We'll take the bus home. Someone will bring you back tomorrow to pick up your car, won't they, Rob?"

He doesn't answer.

"What do you think, Chad?" Officer Bartlett says to Mr. Ho. "Should we arrest them or just make a report?"

"We can make a report if they get on the next bus."

Maybe they're playing good cop/bad cop. I don't care. I'll play along. I'll play dumb, as long as they don't arrest me. The last thing I want is a police record. Especially after what Nicole's been through.

"Give me your name for the report, young lady," Officer Bartlett says as she flips open a leather-covered book.

"Sandee Elizabeth Mason. I was only trying to stop him from driving drunk."

"And disturbing the peace," Officer Bartlett writes on the form in her book.

"Who are you, young man?" Mr. Ho asks.

"Rob."

"Rob Mason," Officer Bartlett says slowly as she writes the name in triplicate.

"No, he's—"

Rob shakes his head, and I turn my words into a cough.

"Use your sleeve, missy. That could be contagious, and I'm not taking it home to my kids."

"Sorry," I say again. I hate Rob's pretending to be a Mason, but I'll handle it later, when we're alone.

Mr. Ho says, "Give your little sister the keys, and we'll let you go, but remember that your names will be on file with BART and the police. If there are any further incidents, the report will be used against you."

"Thanks for understanding," I say, though they understand nothing. It almost kills me to say, "Come on, big brother. The bus is here."

Its motor rumbles, which is a good thing, because Rob keeps saying, "You're not my little sister. You're one hot chick" as I get him on board and into a seat.

We're out of Walnut Creek and heading down San Ramos Boulevard when Rob says, "Gimme my keys, Sandee."

"Not until we're at your house."

"You get off first."

"Fine. I'll give them to you when I get off. How many beers did you have?"

"Not many."

"How many?"

"Four." He giggles. Then he laughs and laughs, but his eyes fill with tears after I ask him what's so funny.

"Four 22-ouncers, little sis. Don't tell 'Mom and Dad,' okay, sis?"

I do the math and say, "Do you know that's over a six-pack?"

"Do I care?"

"You will if anybody finds out. Is this why Nicole broke up with you?" He's being a jerk, but I figure there'll never be a better time to ask.

"She didn't break up with me. I broke up with her."

"Okay," I say, and I draw the word out because I know it isn't the truth.

"I need you to believe me, Sandee. I need somebody to believe me." The tears spill over, and he looks away.

"I'm not going to tell anybody anything. Is that clear enough for you?" I stare at the shadowy trees swaying gently over the streetlamps.

"Please," he says, gripping my arm. "Please be on my side. You don't know what it's like to be so alone."

"You're not alone," I say. "You've got a whole cast full of friends."

"She shouldn't have gotten sober," he says a minute later. "First Bri went away, and then Nicole left me. Senior year's turned into a real bummer. If I died in Afghanistan, nobody would. . . " His lids slide over his eyes. A minute later he's snoring.

When we get close to San Ramos High, I nudge him. He snores louder. "Rob, the keys are in your hand. Can you walk home from the bus stop?"

"Huh?"

I pull the cord so the bus will stop. "Keys are in your hand," I say more insistently.

"You coming, young lady?" the bus driver calls.

"Call me when you get home." There's no response. I tell the driver, "The guy sleeping back there gets off in two more stops. Can you wake him when you get there?"

He shakes his head and says, "Kids."

"Please. It's important."

"You're too young to know what's important. Now go home. I have a schedule to follow."

A mixture of fear and adrenaline surges through me as I get off the bus. I went to a dorm on a UC campus, and I almost got arrested at Walnut Creek BART. Rob won't remember, and I won't forget.

"What's going on, Bri?" I ask as I turn onto our sycamore-lined street. Am I talking to Bri the way Tessa talked to her dad? I'll have to ask if her dad ever answers her when I see her again.

CHAPTER THIRTY

THE HOUSE IS DARK when I put my key in the door. I don't want to turn on a light, so I shine the little flashlight on my keychain around the living room. Mom has fallen asleep on the sofa. She and Dad got home after I left, and I am lucky that she's asleep. Dad is too. His snores rattle the walls. Maybe they trust that I'm in my room.

Sooner or later I'll tell them I delivered the letter, but right now, I'm afraid I'd say something about Daniel, and that would upset everybody all over again. They can't face up to Bri's death, and I don't want to make it worse.

I tiptoe upstairs. "Don't spend the night on the bus, Rob," I say as I brush my teeth. The face in the mirror nods. I huddle under the covers waiting for his call. It doesn't come at 11—or 11:15—or 11:30.

"What is your problem, Rob?" I text him, but he doesn't write back. Not that I expect him to.

I hear Mom coming up the stairs. She stops by my door, and I turn over and sigh loudly enough that she'll know I'm here. As soon as she hears me, she walks away.

I dream about explosions in the sand again and fireworks streaming through the darkened sky. When I open my eyes, the sun is rising behind Pine Mountain.

I look for Rob at brunch. I ask Nicole and Tessa and even Diego if they've seen him. No one has. Maybe he's too hungover for school. Maybe he's still riding the same BART bus—or maybe Ms. G wrote him an excuse so he could do something for the show. We only have four more rehearsals until tech week, when we'll add all the lighting and sound cues and run the whole show without stopping. That goes on until Thursday, which is opening night. I've heard horror stories about tech week, and I can't wait to find out who's going to yell and what they'll yell about.

At the start of third period, Dr. Henderson's secretary makes a special announcement over the PA system. "Will the cast and crew of *Oklahoma!* please report to the rehearsal room at the beginning of lunch? We repeat, the cast and crew of *Oklahoma!* is to report to the rehearsal room at the beginning of lunch."

I lean over to Diego, who sits next to me in World Cultures, and say, "What's that all about?"

"Search me. Why don't you ask your boyfriend, Rob?"

"He's not my boyfriend, and besides, he's not here today, remember?"

"Please give me your attention, Sandee," Ms. Martin says, but I can't think about World Cultures. I fake it and pretend I'm listening even though I don't know whether one of the leads has broken an arm or gotten in a car crash or been kidnapped. Sometimes faking it is a lot like acting, except I'm in real life and have no script to follow.

When the lunch bell rings, I head for the rehearsal room. Who needs lunch? I'll survive on some old M&Ms at the bottom of my backpack. Rob is across the room, lounging on the Senior Sofa, but Nicole sits in the middle of the room, far away from his whole senior crowd. Jenn, Diego, and a few guys from the band hang out with me near Ms. G's desk.

Ms. G and Mr. Jackson stand in front of the stage with Mrs. McMurphy, the choreographer. All three of them have their arms folded. Dr. Henderson walks in, and no one is smiling as Ms. G says, "Please give us your attention. A serious problem has come up."

"What?" Stephanie asks.

Ms. G ignores her, even though she's one of the leads. "We've had a theft. Someone stole the guns we borrowed from Major Gregory."

"How could someone—" I hear Jenn whisper. Diego shushes her.

"You've got to be kidding," Tessa murmurs. She stands next to me, clutching her backpack and shaking her head.

Ms. G holds her hand up to stop us, and Dr. Henderson says, "People, please," in his booming baritone.

"I'm not finished," Ms. G says. "We're very concerned. This is a serious betrayal of trust."

The cast starts to protest.

"I'll take it from here." Dr. Henderson's eyes are hard. "We don't know who has possession of these guns or how they might be planning to use them. I've notified the police. You may have seen them searching the campus, but the guns are still missing. If they'd found them, we wouldn't be here right now. We need your help, and you need those firearms. I know you've worked hard, and I don't want to cancel your show, but I will if we don't get the guns back. Is that clear?"

I look at Diego, who's looking at Jenn. Her eyes fill with tears.

Rob stands up and says, "When we left the theater, the guns were secured in the props cabinet, right, Sandee?"

"Absolutely."

"You locked the cabinet, didn't you?" he asks.

A chill runs through me. Of course I locked the cabinet. He double-checked it. So why is he asking this in front of everyone?

"Don't even start, Rob," Nicole says before I can answer. She glares, and he rolls his eyes.

Tessa says, "What is wrong with you, Rob? I saw her put them away and check the lock. There's no reason in the world Sandee would steal from this show."

"I'm not saying she stole them. I'm saying that Sandee took care of them."

"Rob, you and I were the last two people to leave the theater," Ms. G says.

"The guns were secured and so was the theater."

"Right."

Rob's forehead glistens. It's getting hot in here.

"I checked the padlock myself, but not the contents, and no one has borrowed my keys in the last twenty-four hours. So if anyone saw or heard anything suspicious, we need to know about it. We have to get to the bottom of this. You heard Dr. Henderson. There might not be a musical, and no one here wants that."

Diego raises his hand and says, "Do you think the jocks did it to put the drama geeks out of business?"

"No, and you shouldn't categorize people that way."

"It doesn't make sense though, Ms. G. Who would do this to us?" Jenn asks, dabbing at her eyes.

"Who could break through the school's security?" Stephanie asks.

"Who knows the code?" one of the dancers calls out.

"No students," Ms. G says. "The guns were here when we left."

"Is everybody in the show here?" Dr. Henderson asks.

Mr. Jackson holds up his clipboard. "Perfect attendance for once."

"The police will be back later today to look at the security cameras, so if anybody knows anything or saw anything, please come forward. Stealing firearms is serious, and this has to stop or this school will never do another show that requires weapons. Your teacher told me she trusted you and talked me into letting you use disabled firearms. I hope you earn our trust back."

He walks out, and a minute later, everyone in the room bursts into protests.

Rob stands up and says, "Come on, you guys, think. Who's been against this show? Who's against San Ramos Drama?" When he doesn't get an answer, he adds, "What if the show's canceled and the guns turn up afterwards?"

"That would be very sad after all the hard work everybody's put in. There isn't another two-weekend slot on the calendar for the rest of the year. I'm not sure there's even one weekend with a Thursday, Friday, and Saturday free."

"Is rehearsal still happening?" Jenn asks.

"Yes. Be here at 3:30 today. We have to be ready if those weapons are found."

The word *weapons* makes me shudder. "So, where should we look for the guns?"

"Maybe you should listen more than look," Rob says before Ms. G can answer.

"Watch Facebook," Jenn adds. She can be such a ditz.

"Check every storage locker in the place," Diego says. "Could we do that? Can we search the campus ourselves?"

"It's already been done by the professionals, Diego. If you know of a place that might not have been searched, tell Dr. Henderson or me, and we'll get word to the police. Otherwise, use your visual and auditory powers of observation. You have ten minutes left of your lunchtime, so you better get going."

Who would sabotage drama? Most of the school doesn't even notice us.

I sit on a bench outside the rehearsal room and go on Facebook from my iPhone. Postings from some of the cast are already there. "Help us find the show's missing guns," Jenn says on both her page and the school's page.

I look at Diego's post: "How would you like it if we stole your things? Nobody likes a thief."

"You got what you deserved," V. S. Dante says.

"Who is V.S. Dante?" I ask.

Diego wouldn't know. Rob might, but Nicole is going past so I ask her, "Do you know someone named V. S. Dante?"

She shakes her head and keeps walking. A second later, she turns back and says, "Why?"

I show her the post, and she says, "Show Ms. G right now."

I can't believe her seriousness. "It's Facebook," I say.

"Come on, Sandee. It could help. I'll go with you if you want."

We show it to Ms. G, who goes to her computer and says, "I'll check the school's records and talk to Dr. Henderson," but a minute later she says, "There's no one in the whole school with the last name of Dante."

"Check the profile," Nicole says to me.

"He graduated from here and is now a student at Pine Mountain College. Works at Safeway. No friends listed."

"No friends?" Nicole asks. "I'll bet the profile's either brand new or a fake. Why is someone stalking our drama department?"

This is creepy. I'll take my dramas onstage, thank you. Whoever is playing the role of Dante on Facebook needs to be stopped.

CHAPTER 33

Dear Bri,

OMG! I need your help so much.

I know it's ridiculous to write you an e-mail, but I have to talk to somebody who'll listen. You are listening, aren't you? Even if you aren't, I have to get this out.

I don't get what's going on with the show right now. For that matter, I don't know what's happening with you. What happened to all the encouragement you used to give me?

Let me just tell you what's happening, okay?

Rob tried to pick me up at BART after I delivered your letter to Emma. I guess he was trying to be nice, but he was drunk. Seriously drunk! No way I was going to get in a car with him.

I couldn't get him to give me his keys, and the BART police called the real police, and they threatened to arrest us. The only good part was that Mom and Dad don't know.

Okay, I'm worried about the show and Rob, but what I really want to know is what happened with Emma? Did you break up with her or did she break up with you? Did you agree to see other people or did Afghanistan change you?

I have so many questions. Can you see us here? Can you

go back and see things that have already happened, like the moment when somebody took something?

Today we found out that the revolvers I borrowed from Major Gregory are gone. Remember when you and Rob used to play practical jokes on him?

Well, this is no joke. Dr. Henderson and Ms. G think someone stole them, and if we don't find them, the show's going to get canceled.

Who would steal a revolver? Sorry. Bad question— especially after the way you died. Besides, we may know who stole it. Somebody named V. S. Dante. The trouble is that no one has ever heard of him. He posted on Facebook that we got what we deserved. So I decided to Google "Dante + Contra Costa County." Nobody has that last name.

So I asked Jenn if someone could make up names and bios on Facebook.

She said you could make up a name but you needed an e-mail address. I know Google gives them out free. Now that I think about it, Facebook has actors and musicians on their site and you can tell they didn't sign themselves up.

I don't know how it works up there, but if you're watching us, you already know the police couldn't figure out who did this, so it's up to us.

Can you tune in to what's already happened, like we tune in to reruns, and let me know what you see? I know it sounds silly, but you talked to me through Madame Naomi, and it had to be you because she didn't know your dog was named Spike or you had a friend named Rob.

I know I'm asking you to read minds and that's probably not fair, but do you know who wants the show canceled? Do you know what's wrong? Can you tell me, please?

For that matter, do you know what's going on with Rob? His moods flip around all the time, and last night he reeked of beer. Did you ever drink with him? Don't be shocked. I know everybody does it in high school, and just in case you're wondering, no, I'm not everybody.

When Rob came to BART to pick me up and the police showed up, he told them his name was Rob, and they assumed he was my big brother, Rob Mason. He thought it was a big joke.

Do you still have eyes, or do you interpret things in some other way? I want to help him, but how? What do you know that I can't see here?

Okay, Bri. This isn't working. Maybe you need to read this before you can answer. I'd send it out into the universe, but you don't have an e-mail address anymore. I think I'll save it in my Drafts folder. You don't even have a computer, but your old one is still in your room. Mom won't let anybody touch it. I don't really blame her. We miss you a lot, Bri, which reminds me. . .

The principal wants to honor servicemen at a special assembly. I have less than a week to put together a PowerPoint and a speech about you and help find the missing revolvers.

Can you let me know if I'm close to finding them? Can you at least whisper "You can do it" in my ear?

Love from your maturing sister,

I cross it out and write *Love,*
I think of Emma and cross it out and write *Missing you, Sandee*

CHAPTER THIRTY-TWO

I GAZE IN THE mirror propped in front of my laptop, smile like Jenn, and whisper, "Rob, I need to talk to you."

No. That sounds needy—but it's true. I hate my forced smile. "Rob, I need to talk to you about Bri. Please. I need your help."

I sound more needy, not less.

"Rob, I need your help because you knew Bri better than any of us."

A March wind whishes through the tree next to the window, and a shower of walnut petals falls to the ground. *Bri? Are you there?*

I don't hear him. Just in case, though, I ask, "Why am I rehearsing for a conversation with Rob?"

There's no answer. I don't need one. Girls rehearse when they're going to call a boyfriend. Rob's not my boyfriend. He's the stage manager. I'm his assistant and a girl he flirts with sometimes—but not his girlfriend.

Every time we talk about Bri, he folds in on himself. I don't understand it.

Maybe if I ask him after rehearsal. "Your homework, Sandee?"

"I'm sorry, Miss Bowen. I didn't realize we started. I was thinking."

"I noticed." She runs her fingers along the edge of my desk, and I see the age spots on her knuckles again. "Were you thinking about algebra?"

"Well, I was thinking about relationships, and algebra is about the relationships of numbers, isn't it?"

A couple of juniors in the back laugh out loud.

"Your homework please?" she asks at the same time one of the clowns behind me calls out, "No comeback, Miss Bowen?"

"Say that again, Jamie, and I'll write a referral."

I open the cover of my book and hand her my homework, which is folded in half. I guess I should call it my attempted homework. Half the time I don't know what we're talking about in here. The other half of the time, I don't know how it applies to my life. Maybe if I were going to program computers or work in a chem lab, it would matter, but I'm going to pursue the arts in some form, even if I never get a role.

I actually feel sorry for Bowen. She has been teaching way too long. Everybody knows it. She's waiting to retire like we're waiting for graduation. Ooo! That would make a good analogy for English.

"Sandee, would you put the first problem on the board?" Miss Bowen asks as she puts a giant paper clip around our homework.

"Can I have my paper back?"

"Do it from the book, and explain each step as you go."

I hate that line. She says she wants to see if we've understood the work, but I think she does it to find out who's copying.

I take my book to the front of the room. "Hope I'm not wasting everybody's time."

"We'll risk it," she says like she knows she has nailed me.

Fine. Your classroom. Your show. I pick up a green pen from the stash in the cup on her desk and copy the problem on the whiteboard.

I stare at it. I did my homework as the sun rose over the ridge this morning, and now I can't remember a thing. I'm like the actor who's onstage and doesn't know his lines. I sigh and say, "Can I use the notes I took in class?"

"Try it without notes. Pretend you're playing the role of a geometry student whose grade is on the line."

Ouch! That was not nice.

Nicole and a couple of the others giggle. Nicole's taking this class because she was out of school last fall. She hates math as much as I do, and I don't know why she's laughing at me.

I begin writing and explaining. The two sides of the equation are like a seesaw. Things rebalance with each step. The class is my audience, and I'm the storyteller.

When Miss Bowen says, "Good job, Sandee," I consider it a glowing review. Then she says, "You do fine when you concentrate," which bursts my bubble. I'm off the hook for the day, and as I sit down, I continue thinking about Rob and Bri and my speech.

Right before rehearsal, I spot Rob texting on the back steps outside the rehearsal room. I take a breath, walk up, and say, "I need to talk to you about growing up with Bri. Can we do it after rehearsal?"

"Why?"

"'Cause you knew him better than anybody else."

"Is this about that speech?"

"Please, Rob. I need your help."

Ms. G sticks her head out the door and tells him to get everyone inside.

She has given him a perfect excuse to avoid me.

Today, we're running the whole show with no interruptions except for the normal fifteen-minute intermission between Acts One and Two. Nicole, Jenn, and most of the other girls wear character shoes and twirl in rehearsal skirts. Diego and the other boys put on cowboy hats and strap on empty holsters.

Rob holds the prompt book, and I proofread the program because I can do it at the same time I watch the stage-right props table. Too bad I can't see what's going on around the stage-left table. I'd ask Tessa to watch it, but she has the set pieces to worry about, and I can't ask Diego because he's onstage. I miss working with a cast I can trust.

How could anybody sneak revolvers out of the rehearsal room? Did they use a gym bag or reuse Major Gregory's duffel bag?

My concentration is gone. I start proofing the program again.

At the end of Act One, Rob says, "Curtain warmers, up" into his headset a second before Ms. G says, "May I see everyone in the house?"

I know what she's going to say: "Where's the energy? Where are the objectives?" She surprises me. She looks up and down the row of actors and techies sitting along the edge of the stage. Diego stares at his feet. Nicole's gaze is fixed on the back wall. "I thought we were going to rise above the missing guns," Ms. G says.

Nicole nods. So does Jenn, but Diego says, "Isn't rehearsing a little ridiculous if Henderson's going to shut us down?"

"Absolutely not. If we quit, whoever stole those revolvers gets his way," Nicole states.

"Or *her* way." Rob glares at her with eyes so fierce that her friends look away. "It could have been a disgruntled actress, you know. There are a lot of them out there."

Nicole folds her arms, and I admire her restraint.

"Rehearsing is like taking the high road, isn't it, Ms. G?" Jenn asks.

"It will be if you get back in character, remember your objectives, and put appropriate amounts of joy and tension into each moment. Are we still an ensemble?" Ms. G asks.

"Yes."

"Louder," Diego calls out. His eagerness surprises me.

"Yes!"

"With conviction," Rob shouts. For once, I don't mind his flipping moods.

"Yes!" we all answer. We've talked ourselves into it. The show matters again. The second act sparkles, and I think our audience, including the people from Pine Mountain College, will love it.

After the company sings the finale, I hear Rob say, "Lights out. Go." He whispers, "One-two-three-four-five-six-seven-eight-nine-ten" as the cast exits with rustling petticoats and shuffling boots. "Curtain warmers, ready. Curtain warmers, go." He doesn't even pause between the two or remove his headset before he adds, "If the police can't find those revolvers, we should do it ourselves. Who hates drama? Who are the troublemakers?"

If anyone answers, they don't do it over the headset.

After Ms. G's comments, which include more praise than usual, Rob asks, "Are we going to let a bunch of outsiders walk all over us? No way."

"No way," the cast shouts back. We sound like we're at a basketball rally. Ms. G says, "Rob, please," but we drown her out. All of us, together, shout, "No way. No way!" The cast sounds like an army marching to the dressing rooms. Backstage, I slide the props onto their correct shelves, and Tessa stores the set pieces. She isn't chanting. She isn't even smiling. Has she finally heard something about her sister or does she hate cheerleaders and pep rallies?

CHAPTER THIRTY-THREE

WHEN I ASK TESSA what's wrong, she tells me, "Chanting is mindless."

"I never thought of that." Tessa's right, but it energizes me and makes me feel like I'm part of a cause that matters.

I carry my excitement all the way home, and once I'm there, I go back to work on the PowerPoint for the assembly. In Mom's old scrapbooks I find photos of Boy Scouts and baseball and birthdays. One of Bri's middle school teachers brought a class photo by the house and asked if we wanted it. Now I add it in.

I scan yearbooks for photos of him doing student government projects, and I put his graduation photo with Emma into the collection because it's way better than telling people how she humiliated him.

I like the photos, but I can hear my new English teacher saying, "Do the pictures tell a story?"

Not yet, I think, but what is the story I'm trying to tell? Dr. Henderson wants me to talk about who he was before high school, but that doesn't tell the whole story. Who was he?

He was a good guy who died too soon.

He had a promising future, but he died too soon. People respected and loved him, but he died too soon.

Duh! I think. The theme is staring me in the face.

He died too soon.

I need pictures of him in uniform. I need pictures of him walking into the fate that no one wanted for him, and I need to go into the footlocker again to see what he sent home.

I go to Bri's room and kneel next to his footlocker. This time the TV downstairs covers the squeaking hinges as I lift the lid. The padlock is gone. Maybe Dad took it off once he saw the note to Emma was missing. Maybe he's giving me silent permission to search through Bri's stuff—or maybe Bri took it away, somehow, even though he's gone.

I lift the lid and see the same uniforms in the same order. Bri probably had a backpack, but it blew up when the IED obliterated him.

I remove the desert camouflage pants and jackets and lay beige T-shirts on top of them. I dig deeper. I'm on a mission to find pictures of his final days.

I only know who he was here at home, so I send a text to student government, whose e-mail address I still remember, and one to the current track team: "Do you have memories of Brian Mason? Please write back."

Rob texts, "A bunch of us are having a before-tech-week party. Can it wait?"

"No," I type and hit send. Who does he think he is? He isn't in Student Council, and he certainly doesn't run track. Who showed it to him?

A couple minutes later, someone's ringing the doorbell. I race downstairs, but Dad gets there first. Tessa and Diego are both standing in our hall.

"Did you send your text to half the world?" Diego asks as he comes in and plops on the sofa facing our big-screen TV.

I'm afraid Dad will ask, "What text?" but instead he excuses himself and goes into the kitchen.

"Just the people who knew Bri, I thought," I whisper.

"Well, I got it from the music commissioner, and he wasn't even in band," Diego says.

"Everybody is forwarding it," Tessa says.

What have I done?

"Bri and I both ran track when I was a sophomore and he was a junior," Tessa says. "He always got there early so he could warm up. I don't remember a lot of kids watching him, but that girl . . . Emma, I think?"

I nod. Little does she know.

"Emma was there a lot, and Rob would sometimes stop on his way home. They'd hang out next to the chain-link fence, and Bri would wave to them both, but he never looked over at them when he did it."

"How . . . ?"

She puts up a hand to stop me. "The coach asked him once how he managed that, and he said he used his peripheral vision. It's not much of a story, but it's about all I remember."

"So he saw everything, and not just what was in front of him?" I open up "Reminders" on my iPhone and write it down.

Diego's feet won't stop jiggling. "Can we see the PowerPoint? It might help me remember the Saturdays when we spied on him and Rob."

I plug my laptop into the TV, lower the lights, and start the PowerPoint on our flat-screen TV. I run the slides with some songs that Mom and Dad suggested last week. They make it more tear-jerky and inspirational, and I hope nobody will get embarrassed or laugh. About halfway through, I hear a loud sniff. I can't tell if it's Tessa or Diego. Neither one moves.

My PowerPoint ends with a shot of Bri's military equipment and "The Wind Beneath My Wings," which sounds corny, but I didn't do it for the kids. I did it for Mom and Dad, and I'm pretty sure Bri would approve. This is the story of who he became, but no one will know why unless I figure it out and add slides that show the world how he became a soldier.

"You know how eulogies are always about who a person was?"

Tessa asks as I bring up the lights. "This is about who he's becoming
. . . was becoming."

"Wow, Tessa. Last night I decided it was about the fact that he
died too soon, but that's better." She shifts in her seat and takes out
a water bottle. I should ask her how she's doing with her PowerPoint
about Kayla, but I turn to Diego and ask, "What do you think?"

He scratches under his nose. He scratches his chin. Finally he
says, "It's good. Maybe it's too good. I still think about Rob and Bri
trying cigarettes when they hung out here on Saturdays. Remember
the wisps of smoke coming out of Bri's window? A bunch of kids will
relate to that."

"That's right. They opened the window even if it was raining."

"At least we never ratted them out."

"We're not going to, either. Mom and Dad will be there," I remind
him. Tessa stares past the screen, and I wish I could read her mind.
"Did we leave anything out?" She shakes her head. "So?"

"Is there anything else Bri would want you to say?"

"Either he'd say the sacrifice was worth it or he'd say take care of
yourself and go to college. I know it was worth it to him when he left
home, but maybe Afghanistan changed him," I say, thinking of Emma.

"You may never know what happened. All you can do is talk
about who he was when he left. Let kids draw their own conclusions."

Diego straightens up, and there's a mischievous look in his eyes.
"Tell about the time you borrowed his allowance and didn't pay it
back and he stole your diary and read it to all the guys on the track
team—or the time he ditched Boy Scouts and made out with that
freckle-faced girl by the canal." Sometimes I think Diego knows our
family a little too well, but what can you expect when you live next
door to someone?

"Okay. I get it, but my parents will hate it if I tell the whole school
about those things."

The doorbell rings again. It's Jenn, standing there in skinny jeans
that show her pale legs through designer holes. Did she even know Bri?

"I got your message, and I didn't want to stay at Rob's party. How can I help?"

"With stories about Bri."

"Got one," she says, sliding onto the sofa between Diego and Tessa. "He was in the seventh-grade spelling bee, and I watched him from the back of the house because they held it at my parents' theater. He was kinda cute, but really quiet, and he looked like his mom picked out his clothes." She snuggles up to Diego until their legs touch. "He did really well, but they gave him a monstrous word when there were only three people left. Maybe they would have given him an easier one if he looked a little less geeky." The story's good, but I can barely pay attention. She's rubbing her leg against Diego's. Tessa and I look at each other as she takes Diego's hand and says, "A girl in the chorus asked me when you're going to get a girlfriend."

Tessa gulps, and says, "Jenn, can you help me get us some soft drinks?"

Diego's eyes plead with me while Jenn and Tessa head for the kitchen. As soon as we're alone I say, "She's got a point. When *are* you going to get a girlfriend?"

Immediately, his face relaxes. His embarrassment is gone. "Maybe soon, if the right girl is interested." He looks straight at me, and he winks as he says it.

"Ask for what you want," I remind him despite the butterflies fluttering in my stomach. The voice is mine, but the words sound like something Bri would say. Is he in my head again, or am I finding my own voice?

CHAPTER THIRTY-FOUR

WHEN I E-MAIL MY latest backstage shots to Ms. G, I ask, "Security tapes show anything?"

She writes back, "They showed nothing, but your rehearsal photos are good. We'll put them in the auditorium lobby with a sign that says *Photos by Sandee Mason.*"

My stomach flutters. Everybody will see them when they walk into the assembly, and then they'll hear me speak, and my head is spinning. "Bri, I'm sorry you're gone, but I love all the attention," I whisper. Selfish me! I'm embarrassed. It's not right to think this way, but there's nothing I can do to bring him back, and if his death somehow brings me a little recognition, I won't run from it.

I lie on my bed, put on my headphones and imagine Bri running around the track. He's the only runner, and I'm the only spectator. He goes slower and slower, and so does the stopwatch in my hand. The sand on the track becomes an endless dune. Rumbling gunfire comes closer, and waves of sand swallow Bri up. Then flashes of fire and fireworks burst into the sky and fade into darkness.

It's 4 a.m. when I wake up. Most of the streetlights are off, and I see millions of tiny stars twinkling in the night sky.

I wake up thinking about the PowerPoint, so I steal into Bri's room. On the bulletin board over his desk, I spot a five-by-seven card that says, "Every puppy should have a boy." The puppy looks over the boy's shoulder. "You like that, Spike?" I ask as I take a picture of it.

When I come home, I often find Spike lying outside the door to Bri's room. He misses his master. I take a picture of Spike, sprawled across the foot of Bri's bed. When I look at, I spot his footlocker in the foreground. I can use it in the PowerPoint. I'll talk about how much Bri loved Spike and how well he cared for him.

I turn back to the bulletin board. Next to the puppy picture is a postcard that says, *Figuring out who you are is the whole point of the human experience.* The words are written in cream-colored letters superimposed on a dense redwood forest. Beneath it is the name Anna Quindlen. Mom has something by her in the bookcase.

It doesn't sound like something Bri would say, so I turn it over and see that Emma sent it during spring vacation of senior year. She toured colleges that week. A lot of the kids did, but Bri had already decided to enlist.

I search his footlocker one more time and find a packet of letters wrapped in royal-blue ribbon. It smells like jasmine. The return address says Azita Fazouli, but the rest of it is written in Arabic characters I can't decipher. If he didn't want anyone to read it, he would have destroyed it, wouldn't he? Most guys don't keep letters. Slowly, I pull out a piece of stationery that's tissue-paper thin. It looks like he saved every letter she ever wrote.

"Dear Brian," Azita wrote in the same precise writing I used when I was first learning cursive. "I think of you often. I lucky to find you. I never thought I love Western man. When will I see you again?"

I slip it back into the envelope, and pull out another. "My family pleased to meet you and now sees you good man. Visit soon again?" Her last letter ends with "I miss you when you go with patrol. Stay safe. Remember me in heart."

Did he tell Azita about Emma—or Emma about Azita? Did he tell Azita about Mom or Dad or me? I shiver in the pale moonlight pouring in through Bri's window—through the window. It isn't really Bri's room anymore, but it isn't anyone else's either.

I can't tell Mom and Dad what I've found, nor can I hide it. Mom wants to remember Bri exactly as he was, so I slip the letters back in the envelope and replace the envelope exactly where I found it in the footlocker.

"I'm glad he met you, Azita," I whisper, even though I know she's halfway around the world. It's hard to imagine my brother walking hand in hand with a dark-eyed girl wearing a Middle Eastern headscarf.

I place his shirts over the letters, and a folded piece of paper falls to the ground. *Sandee Special* is scrawled across it.

I haven't thought about Sandee Specials all year. Starting a recycling center for the neighborhood was a seventh-grade Sandee Special. So was sending my story about our fifth-grade class's Christmas outreach to the local paper.

Helping Bri cover up the fact that he drove before he got a license was a Sandee Special.

I unfold the paper and read,

Sandee, if you find this, I want you to know that you can be anybody you want to be. Even a soldier. If that's what you want. Rob and I spent a lot of time putting you down, and I hope it didn't hurt you. It's just what big brothers do.

We're about to go out on another mission, and sometimes when I see the sad eyes of the kids here, I think about the way you looked at me when we called you a punk and a loser.

Trust yourself. You can be anybody you want to be. Make your own decisions. Trust your instincts. I know I made the decision to come here, but I did it because Dad convinced me that being a soldier is what a man does. Now I'm not so sure. I'm not afraid to fight for my country, but if I don't make it back, I want you to do as many Sandee Specials as you can and make the world a better place, okay? And while you're doing it, be happy, and when you find the right guy, don't be afraid to fall in love.

Don't settle for just anybody.

Take care of Mom, Dad, Spike, and Rob. He needs to know he's got a place where he belongs.

FYI, we have a cool family. It's much easier to see when you're away from home.

And take care of your boyfriend if you ever get one. Just kidding. I'll bet you already have one. Be sure he's worthy of you. Love, Bri

My throat tightens as I refold the note. It's not going back in the footlocker. I'm on my way back to bed when I see one more quote on Bri's bulletin board: *Life is what happens to you while you're busy making other plans.* ~ *John Lennon.* I snap a picture for the PowerPoint. It sums up Bri's life in a way I never could.

I have to be up at 6:15. After school, we'll have the infamous tech rehearsal I've heard so many horror stories about. All I have to do is preset the props, and I've been doing that for a while, so I'm not worried about anything except the missing guns as I crawl back into bed.

When I wake up, a dream about guns and petticoats and character shoes slides away before I can figure it out.

CHAPTER THIRTY-FIVE

WHAT IF ROB KNOWS about Azita and that's why he won't answer my questions? What if he's trying to protect Bri's memory? I think about that as I head for English.

Diego comes rushing up to me with news. "Your rehearsal photos are hanging in the lobby. Your name's on them, and they look absolutely fabulous."

"Already?"

"I saw them when I helped Mr. Jackson move the drums into the orchestra pit. You're going to be famous."

Sometimes I love the way he exaggerates. "You're awesome," I say, and he actually blushes before he takes off for his computer class.

I sneak into my seat in English two seconds before the bell rings. My brain is already on overload, and it's only Monday.

Mrs. Marron has written *Death of a Soldier* on the board, and it makes me cringe. Everywhere I turn there are reminders. Then she says, "We're going to read an American tragedy that's considered a classic, Arthur Miller's *Death of a Salesman.*" OMG! I can't even read right anymore. It says salesman—not soldier.

Sometimes I wonder if it would be better to be Tessa and still have hope or better to accept Bri's fate and move on. I get a headache as we start reading the play, and I don't lose it until school's out.

Musicians are tuning up in the orchestra pit when I walk into the auditorium for Monday's rehearsal. On Saturday, we hauled all the set pieces over, including the surrey. We set everything up, taped the stage, and stored all the set pieces backstage. Before we left, Rob lit a ghost lamp and placed it downstage right. I can't decide if I love or hate that name. A ghost lamp sounds like something we'd light to remember Bri, but I can't think about that now.

I walk in on Rob calling the light cues so Ari, a lighting tech, can practice. Downstairs in the dressing room, a few actors sit in front of lit mirrors, putting the assigned color of base on their faces. One of the costumers pins the waist of Diego's pants. His cowboy costume makes him look old fashioned. He puffs on the corncob pipe we found in Berkeley, and I almost see real smoke coming out of it.

"You were right, Sandee," he says when he sees me reflected in the mirror.

"About what?"

"About acting. It feels awesome."

My eyes are misty, but Diego put his lips next to my ear and whispers, "I really wish you had a part. You deserve it more than I do." Then he looks around, sees the room's empty except for the girl with pins between her lips, and gives me a quick kiss. "That was private," he tells her, and she grins.

I know this is corny, but I finally understand why romance stories talk about throbbing hearts. I put my arms around Diego and kiss him back, long and slow. "You're very special," I whisper.

"Cord Elam thanks you for your help, and so do I."

Don't hide behind Cord Elam! I want to shout. I don't. It would ruin the moment. Instead I say, "I have to sweep the stage."

Upstairs, Ms. G shows me the starter pistols she borrowed from PE. They don't look as bad as I expected, but the handles are clearly plastic.

Where are the guns I brought in? If we wind up on the news because some psycho kid stole them and turned them back into weapons, no one in San Ramos Drama will ever live it down.

Rob comes up and hands me my headset. He lurches and grabs the edge of the props table, but he straightens right up. Maybe he's tired—or maybe he has been drinking. I look into his eyes, but he only says, "Go over there so I can test it."

Nicole swishes by, carrying her makeup case and wearing a sweet smile.

Jenn follows, swinging her own makeup case. Her smug grin makes me want to puke. As she passes me, she whispers, "This is so exciting. I can't wait to see how I look in costume." She sounds like a third grader who's about to put on her butterfly costume at the children's theater.

How would she look in my headset? I wonder as I push down the red button and say, "Testing. Testing."

"Good job, Sandee," Rob answers.

I pushed the button again. "Rob, any chance you could answer the questions I sent you about Bri?"

"I don't have time right now. Let's go out after the show, and do it then."

"Fine, but we're running out of time."

Instead of answering, he says, "Would you go to the dressing rooms and tell the actors that it's fifteen minutes to places?"

I hurry down the dimly lit stairs. The grooved walls and wooden stairs remind me of a scene in a Nancy Drew mystery where Nancy goes through a secret door and down a back staircase.

A blanket splits the brightly lit dressing room into two sections: one for boys and one for girls; everyone keeps crossing over, of course. Boys' costumes hang on a rack by the door. Girls' costumes are at the far end. The lights around each makeup station give a warm glow.

"Where's the blush?" a girl calls.

"Does anybody have some pins?"

"My boots are tight."

Nicole slides mascara onto her lashes and asks Jenn, "Will the director from Pine Mountain be here opening night?"

"I'm beginning to wish he weren't coming."

"I hope you don't mean that."

"Not really, but those starter pistols look stupid, and some of the boys sound juvenile when they say their lines."

Nicole stares at her pale face. "I'd love a part on a college campus this summer. It would be awesome to hang out with serious actors."

No one notices me when I shout, "Fifteen minutes to places," so I repeat myself in my loudest voice.

"Thanks, Sandee," Diego calls from the far side of the curtain.

"Yeah! Thanks, Sandee," Nicole chimes in.

I can barely hear her because Rob's yelling through the headset, "Sandee, I need you backstage right this minute."

What now? I race up the stairs. Maybe all this exercise will help my legs look long and sexy.

"I want you to help us swing the house around during the set changes," Rob says the minute I appear. "We need more muscle on the job, and you're the only one available."

"Okay, but it's in place now."

"I know. I need your help during. Set. Changes." He over-articulates the last three words. "Are you deaf?"

"Don't talk that way, Rob. Ensemble, remember?" Angry veins bulge from his neck when he hears my words. "Anything else?" I ask with extreme maturity even though I want to say, "What's your problem, lame ass?"

"Not as long as you do the job."

"Apology accepted."

Before he can respond, Jenn grabs my arm. "Nicole and I need to see you downstairs right now." Her voice trembles. "You are not going to believe this."

"Believe what?"

"Nicole wants to talk to you before we tell Ms. G. Come on." She drags me offstage and down the stairs.

Nicole stands in front of the shoe rack with her arms folded over her makeup-streaked T-shirt. She points behind the shoes. Two wadded up petticoats sit there.

"So?"

"Pick one up." Nicole steps aside as she speaks.

The ruffled cloth is heavy and solid. Something long and heavy tumbles onto the ground. All three of us look around because it makes a huge clatter, but everyone's too busy getting ready for the show to notice.

"Do you believe this?" Nicole asks.

"Oh. My. God. No way!"

"There's another one in my petticoat. We found two out of three."

My heart is in my throat as I stare at the gun, and my pulse races. "How did the police miss them?"

"Maybe they weren't here then?" Nicole's lips tighten to a thin crease.

"So tell Ms. G they're back and let her announce it to the cast," I suggest.

"No way. Don't you see? They're wrapped in *our* petticoats. Jenn's and mine. When Ms. G finds out about them, she'll say we stole them, and you can guess what's going to happen then." Nicole's eyes glisten too brightly.

Ms. G's proud of Nicole's recovery, so I don't really understand. "Which one of you found them?"

"I did," Jenn says, "but don't you see? Somebody wrapped them in *our* petticoats."

When Nicole sees the blank look on my face, she adds, "Somebody wants it to look like we're the ones sabotaging this show. I don't know if it's because I came back or somebody thinks Jenn has too much influence because of her parents, but we both have a lot at stake. That's why *you* have to tell her, Sandee."

"Or you could put them on the props table and say they appeared while you were away from the table." Jenn's eyes shine with hope, but Nicole shakes her head.

The dressing room is nearly empty. Most of the actors have gone upstairs to warm up with Mr. Jackson. We have less than two minutes until curtain.

"Can you imagine the chaos if I take these upstairs without anybody knowing anything?" I ask them both. I look around, but there's no security camera. I guess parents would object to someone recording their kids while they change clothes.

"Oh my God. You're right. Somebody's framing all three of us. We can't just say they appeared," Jenn says.

Rob's voice blares in my earpiece. "Act One places, everybody. Sandee, please cue any actors who are still downstairs. Act One places."

"Ms. G has to know about this first," I whisper. "What if someone found a way to turn our rehearsal into a massacre?" I push the red button on my headset and pull the mike up to my mouth. "Ms. G, are you there?"

"What is it, Sandee? We're about to start."

"Please come down to the girl's dressing room. It's urgent."

"Is someone ill?"

"No, but please come down. We want to show you—"

The first notes of the overture ring out from the orchestra pit. "The show must go on. Whatever it is, it will keep."

"Act One, places," Rob calls. "Places, everyone."

"It's too late now."

Jenn groans, and Nicole shakes her head.

"We'll let everyone know at intermission and use the guns in the second act. That's the best I can do."

Over the headset, Rob shouts, "Places, Sandee. You're screwing everything up."

"Places!" My voice echoes off the dressing room walls.

"Sandee, get backstage right now and do your job," Rob barks. I want to say, "Yes, mein fuhrer. Mein uber jerky fuhrer."

The musicians segue into their next song. I'm tempted to put the guns out and see what happens, but that would make me as bad as Rob.

"What should I do, Bri?" I whisper. I hear the overture blithely playing, "Everything's up to date in Kansas City. . . " Too bad we can't bring everything up to date here.

CHAPTER THIRTY-SIX

BOYS IN GINGHAM SHIRTS and girls in prairie skirts stand in the wings watching the stage lights come up. When the follow spot hits Curley, he opens his mouth and sings, "There's a bright golden haze on the meadow," in his lovely, lilting tenor. Jenn sighs softly.

The actors concentrate on their first line, or their first objective, or how to make sure the pins on the costumes stay closed. Only three of us know the guns are back.

I have nothing to do but watch the props tables, which is impossible anyway because there's one on stage right and another on stage left, so I sneak into the darkened house where Ms. G sits alone making notes on a lit clipboard in her lap. I tap her shoulder and say, "I have to talk to you."

"Not now, Sandee. Get backstage where you belong."

"It won't wait."

"I'm the director. Go backstage now." She looks past me at the actors in the first scene, jots down a quick note, and says, "Go!"

My stomach churns as I slip backstage. When Scene One ends, I watch the actors replace their props, then take my place to wheel Aunt Eller's house off while other techies roll the smokehouse on.

"Lights 13, ready. Lights 13, go," Rob says into his headset, and the lights come up on Jud's smokehouse.

Jud crosses to his table, hears a knock on the door, sees a revolver on the table, and gasps without meaning to. It's a revolver—not a starter pistol.

How did it get upstairs and onto his table?

His eyes grow wide as he hears a second knock on the door. "Well, open it, cain't you?" he calls out with an edgy warble that doesn't fit his character at all.

Rob bellows, "Sandee, where did the revolver on the table come from?"

I can't stop trembling. "I didn't put it there."

"Tessa?" he asks.

Ms. G cuts him off. "I'll talk to you at intermission, Sandee. Until then, put your concentration on the show."

I beckon to Tessa, and she comes over. "Did you look at Jud's house before it came on?"

"Everything was in place right before the overture, but there was a starter gun on the table. Where did the revolver come from?"

"A couple of actors found two of them wrapped in their petticoats and stuffed behind the shoes," I whisper.

"Ms. G's never going to believe that."

"I didn't hide them there."

Her eyes fill with sympathy.

"Somebody in this show can't be trusted because no one but us can get backstage."

"Tessa?" an actor whispers, and she goes to help with a torn costume crisis, even though she's not a costumer.

I retreat to the shadows behind the props table, where nobody can see me.

If Ms. G thinks I had something to do with this, I'm going to be in the worst trouble of my whole life. No way they'll let me give my speech on Wednesday if Ms. G tells the principal I mysteriously found the guns during the tech rehearsal. No way I'll ever do another show or make another friend in this school.

I slide down the backstage wall, pull my legs up to my chest, brush the tears from my eyes, try to breathe without trembling, and wait. I don't move again until the Dream Ballet ends the act.

"Curtain warmers, ready," Rob calls over the headset as Jud says the last line of the act. "Curtain warmers, go. House up. End of Act One. Good job for a first dress rehearsal, everyone. Please meet in the house before we go on to Act Two."

Over her headset Ms. G says, "Sandee, see me outside the backstage door right now."

I know what's coming. I sit and lean against the metal railing on the landing and stare at the darkening sky above the hilltops.

"Where did you find that revolver, Sandee?"

"A couple of cast members found them in the dressing room. I tried to tell you, but—"

Ms. G taps her clipboard; I stop speaking. "Two guns were sitting in the dressing room, in plain view of everyone, and you found them?"

"No." I stare at my shoes. I can't explain without involving Nicole, and she'll absolutely die if she's implicated. I can't betray her. I can't even betray Jenn, though she has far less at stake.

"Sandee, talk to me. You're not helping yourself here."

I look at the wooden steps beneath my feet.

"Somebody hid the guns in a couple of petticoats. Who would do that?"

Rob sticks his head out the door, and the backstage lights spill out in a warm glow. "Do you want to talk to the cast, Ms. G?"

She glances through her clipboard. "Tell people I'll give my notes on Act One later. Remind them to keep their energy up, hang their costumes in the right places, and return their props. How far into intermission are we, Rob?"

"Five minutes. If you and Sandee need to talk, Mr. Jackson and Mrs. McMurphy can give their notes, and I'll handle everything else."

Arrogant bozo. He closes the door. The cool air calms me until Ms. G asks, "If you didn't find the guns, who did?"

I run my hand along the metal pipe by the stairs. I can feel where the paint has peeled away, leaving the metal bare and cold. "I promised them I wouldn't say, but we agreed not to bring them upstairs, so I don't know where the one in Jud's house came from. I swear. Tessa saw a starter pistol on the table when she checked Jud's house before the show."

Ms. G squints. "What happened to the guns in the petticoats?"

"They're downstairs. We wrapped them back up and left them."

"Who showed them to you?"

"No matter how many times you ask, I won't answer." The knots in my stomach tighten.

She sits next to me and runs her teacher eyes over me. I stare at the stars twinkling in the western sky.

"You're making this very difficult, Sandee. If you were me, what would you do?"

That's a tough one, but I'm not about to admit it. "Talk to the whole cast and crew, I guess. Somebody did this, but it wasn't me."

She looks down at her clipboard, then out at the sky above the ridge. "We all know you've been under a lot of stress. Nothing like this has ever happened before. What am I supposed to think?"

"I don't steal. Whoever took those revolvers planted them in Jenn's and Nicole's petticoats to make us look—"

I throw my hand over my mouth. I can't believe I said their names—out loud—after I promised. "I didn't mean that. It slipped out. I'm sorry. Oh my God, I am so sorry."

She glances at her watch. "There's no need to be sorry if you're telling the truth. I'll talk to Jenn and Nicole; maybe they can shed some light on this." Her voice softens. "Sometimes adolescents lie and steal to get attention. Don't you think it's odd that you found the guns just in time to save the show?"

I stare again at the stars above. If Bri is looking down on us, he's probably ashamed of me, unless he's been watching all along and knows I didn't do it. "Please. . . "

"Please what?"

I shake my head, wrap my arms around my legs, and stare at my Top-Siders. Tears splash on them.

"Sandee," she says, and she sounds like she cares again. "Maybe you got jealous of your friends because they have roles. Maybe your parents haven't been paying enough attention since your brother died."

"Why does everybody think that everything I do or don't do has something to do with—" My voice cracks. Tears swim in my eyes. I can't finish.

She holds up her hand, and I stop talking. "I don't want to suspect you. Maybe Rob's right. You're helping him, doing props, taking photos, making phone calls, and maybe we put too much pressure on you."

"Maybe you trust Rob too much. Kids say he used to be a great stage manager, but he's turned into a jerk, and you can't see it." I should stop ragging on her, but I can't. Someone needs to open her eyes.

"Don't say things you don't mean." She stands up and tugs at her pants. "I'll have Rob place the props for the start of Act Two. Don't come in until you've calmed down." She goes inside.

I gasp and gasp, but I can't catch my breath. How did everything get so messed up? The harder I try to stop sobbing, the worse it gets. I'm ready to quit, but I can't. Somebody has to catch the loser who stole our props.

"Shhh."

I look up. No one's there.

"Don't quit," a deep voice whispers.

"Bri?"

"Trust yourself. You know you didn't steal those guns."

The backstage door is cracked open, and I hear the orchestra tuning up. Diego sticks his head out. "Sandee, you doing the props for Act Two?" I try to hide my tear-streaked face in my hands, but he comes down the steps, puts his hands on my shoulders, and gently turns me to him.

I want him to hold me more than anything in the world, but I say, "Don't touch me. I'll get your costume all wet." He pulls me into his chest anyway, and I tell him about Ms. G's accusations.

"Bummer, Sanders."

"How can I prove I didn't steal anything?" He takes my hand, and my pulse quickens. "How are we going to catch him if the police can't?"

"We'll figure it out, Sandee. At least the guns are back, and the show can go on." He's right. He's standing there looking like a mix of masculinity, sexiness, and understanding, and I love that combination. "Come on in, okay? You don't want Rob setting things up for Act Two. The guy has more moods than a mom with PMS." He stands up and offers me both hands. "Don't let some anonymous creep win, okay? We'll figure this out." His "we" is the sexiest word I've heard all night.

CHAPTER THIRTY-SEVEN

DIEGO PUTS HIS ARM around me, and we climb the stairs and walk into the darkened theater together. Lights from the music stands dot the orchestra pit. Mr. Jackson is conducting in the dark. How can anyone follow him?

I put on my headset in time to hear Ms. G say, "Lights up. Now!" Nothing. "Rob, where are you?" He doesn't answer.

Diego sneaks onstage in the darkness. I take my place at the stage-left props table; there's still no way I could watch both sides of the stage at once. Why didn't I tell Ms. G that?

"Rob?" Ms. G asks again.

"It's Sandee. I'm back. Do you want me to go to the booth and call cues?" I ask, even though I know what she'll say.

"Watch the props. Put them away as soon as the actors bring them offstage. Understood?"

"Yes, but what if—"

She talks right over me. "Rob, are you in the building? You've missed the follow spot cues. Where are you?"

Everyone hears static when Rob grabs the headset from its perch above the light board. "Oh my God. Has Act Two started?"

"You don't know?" I almost say, but Ms. G beats me to it.

"Cue 47, go. Cue 48, go. Cue 49, go," Rob says without pausing to breathe. From backstage I see a scramble of light cues blurring into one another. "We're caught up, Ms. G. Sorry about that."

"See me before notes, Rob," she says in the same crisp tone she used with me earlier.

Good. Now maybe he'll get what he deserves.

I stand in silence while the farmer and the cowman sing about being friends in the artificial sunlight. When they start the chorus, I click the button on the headset and whisper, "Tessa, can you keep an eye on the stage-right props table?"

"Until scene changes."

"Quiet, you two," Rob says. Neither one of us says anything. I wonder what Ms. G thinks.

The company performs the rest of Act Two with high Western spirits, despite the lack of light at the start. I notice five more late lighting cues. What is wrong with him? He was fine during the first act.

After the final curtain, Ms. G steps outside with Rob while the rest of us sit on the apron and wait for notes. In less than seventy-two hours, I'm supposed to be standing on this very apron talking about why Bri sacrificed his life for his country.

"Sure am glad someone brought those guns back," Diego says, while I swing my feet against the edge of the stage.

"Could someone have stolen them as a publicity stunt?" Jenn asks.

"I'm not a drama geek, but it's hard to believe this is an inside job," Tessa says quietly.

"Let's pretend the thief is a character," Diego says. "What does he want?" I'm proud of him. Does he even know he's talking like an actor?

"He wants attention," a girl in the chorus says.

"He wants to humiliate the drama kids," the actor playing Jud adds.

"I still say he wants revenge," Rob says. I look behind me and see him standing by the curtain, listening. Ms. G stands next to him.

"You started a good conversation, Diego," Ms. G tells him in front of the whole cast. "Jenn, we're getting notoriety, not publicity. Look up the difference."

"How long have you been standing there?" I ask.

"Long enough to get more perspective," Ms. G says. "I'll give notes before we start tomorrow. Enough has happened for one night. Many of you did some excellent work under challenging circumstances."

Chatter starts. She raises her voice and says, "People, please. One more thing. I'd like to see the heads of every backstage crew before you go. The rest of you put your costumes and props where they're supposed to be, take *all* personal property with you, and I'll see you tomorrow at six."

I put the props away. The two guns in the petticoats are still on the shoe shelf when I decide to take them out of the costume room and lock them in the props cabinet. Ms. G won't listen to me, but whoever put the two guns in the petticoats probably put the third on Jud's table, and if he had all three, that would make him the thief. I hate the way she doesn't trust me anymore, and I ask Tessa and Diego to be my witnesses when I lock the props cabinet.

As Tessa and I walk over to join the other crew heads, she asks, "Are you ready for Wednesday?"

I almost forgot about the speech and Bri during rehearsal, but before I can say so, she turns to Diego, who's trailing us, and says, "Nobody from your family is serving overseas, are they, Diego?"

"A couple of cousins."

"I didn't know that," I say.

"It's okay. They're Arizona cousins, and we don't see them much." Diego knows all about Bri, but he never mentioned his own cousins.

Looking at the broad shoulders stretching out his shirt, I say, "You shouldn't keep secrets from a friend."

"One's in communications, and the other is in shipping. They're not glamour jobs, and they're certainly not in harm's way like Bri was."

I like this new Diego much better than the self-centered clown he used to be.

Ms. G sits on the edge of the apron and says, "Thank you all for staying. Did any of you see anything out of the ordinary backstage while we ran the show? Did you notice any strangers hanging around?"

I know exactly what she's getting at. "Everything seemed normal, but I can't be on both sides of the stage at once." Now she knows I can't watch both props tables at once.

"I didn't see a thing, but no one told me what I should be looking for," Rob says.

Ms. G ignores him and speaks to me. "Nicole and Jenn both say someone took their petticoats away from their costumes, wrapped the revolvers in them, and hid them behind the shoes. Jenn wanted to tell me, but Nicole asked her to wait. Is that right?"

"Yes. Nicole didn't steal them, if that's what you're thinking."

"She's proven herself," Ms. G says quietly.

I see light glinting off something metal, and when I look over at the proscenium arch, Rob's turning a revolver over and examining it closely.

"How did you get that?" I ask. "I locked it up."

"I saw you lock it up," Tessa adds.

Rob laughs. "I found this backstage. Do you even know how many guns you borrowed, little one?"

"Three." I stare into his glazed eyes. "How could I forget a thing like that?"

"Well, maybe somebody brought this in for a scene. It's all rusted over and the firing pin's gone, so I'll put it back where I found it. You don't have to worry about it going off."

"I'll take it," Ms. G said.

He twirls it around, like a gunslinger from the Old West, raises his right arm, and aims it at her. I try to choke back the scream coming out of my mouth, but nothing will hold it in. Between doing the PowerPoint and writing my speech for Wednesday, finding the props and assistant stage managing, and keeping up in five classes, and oh yes, finding out that my brother had been blown up while fighting for freedom and insanity like this, maybe I'm a little too stressed. I'm sure of one thing, though. There's something very wrong with Rob if he's aiming a gun at a teacher, and no one's calling him on it. Not even me. Are we all in a state of shock?

"Only kidding," Rob says as Diego snatches the gun from him and hands it to Ms. G. "Calm down, everybody. Chill. Ms. G knows I wouldn't shoot her."

Ms. G's hands shake as she holds the gun. "That's nothing to kid about, Rob. What's happening to you?"

"Can't anybody take a joke around here?" Rob laughs.

"A joke?" I ask, but Ms. G cuts me off. I can't believe how calm she is.

"Go home, Rob. I don't know what's wrong with you, but this is not acceptable behavior." Half a dozen of us escort her from door to door, double and triple-checking every lock. Afterwards, we all walk out of the auditorium together. Rob's outside, waiting for us. We ignore him. He tails us as we head for the parking lot. We're almost to Ms. G's car when I remember that Rob was going to tell me stories about Bri after rehearsal.

"Are you sure you're okay to drive?" I call to Rob.

"Of course. You need a ride?"

Diego says, "You haven't exactly been yourself tonight. You weren't even on the headset when—"

"I proved I was human. No big deal."

"Okay, Mister Human," I say. "Tell me your favorite story about Bri. Right here. Right now."

"Get in and I will."

"Can Diego come too?"

"Sorry. The back seat's full." He opens the door, climbs into the driver's seat, and stares at me. I can't move. "You want your story or not?"

I peer into the back seat. His car is strewn with everything from basketballs to band equipment. I can't imagine what he is doing with all that stuff, but before I can ask, he says, "I haven't got all night."

I stare up at the moon, which looks like a china plate on a sapphire tablecloth. He rolls down the front windows and says, "Hey, Sandee, did it ever occur to you that war is one big waste?"

Of course it's occurred to me. Has he just figured this out?

He goes on before I can answer, as if he's talking to himself. "Bri shouldn't have gone. We were gonna start a new social network that would match kids up based on ages, interests, and ambitions. It was gonna have photos and music and places to chat with each other— but different from Facebook and Pinterest."

"Can I tell them you two were going to start up a video social network when he got back?"

"Sure. Tell 'em anything you want." He stares at his keys. "I gotta get home."

"Rob, are you okay?"

He looks up, alarmed. "Sure. I'm fine."

"You don't sound like it."

"Get in."

"Were you drinking tonight?" I ask.

"I had Starbucks in the booth. Maybe I have too much caffeine in me."

"Rob, if you have a problem—"

"What I drink is none of your business, and I'm not about to let you rat me out and take my job."

"I don't want your job."

"That's right. I almost forgot." He grips the steering wheel until his knuckles turn white. "You want to be onstage. Well, that's not happening, so get over it."

"Rob, are you drunk?"

"No, and you can walk." He starts his engine, and before I can tell him not to go he says, "Tell them about our social network if you want to. It doesn't matter because it's not happening."

Then he peels out of the parking lot. I look at Diego, who says, "Let him go. A week from now, you'll have your license. In the meantime. . ."

I can't take my eyes off him. His face and neck look like sculptured marble in the moonlight.

"What are you staring at?"

It isn't like me to get all tongue-tied, but I'm overwhelmed by a swelling in my chest and an ache further down. I put my arms around him, and draw his lips to mine. We hold our kiss twice as long as the one in the dressing room. Neither one of us wants it to end.

"Let's go home, and you can practice your speech on me if you want to," he says once we finally pull away.

I want to ask him if he changed the subject because I embarrassed him, but instead I say, "Are you sure you didn't see anybody bring a revolver in or put it on Jud's table?"

"Who can see anything back there? It could have been almost anyone."

CHAPTER THIRTY-EIGHT

ON WEDNESDAY MORNING, I pace behind the closed stage curtain. Butterflies wreak havoc in my stomach. I may never eat again.

The ghost light casts shadows across the sets of *Oklahoma*. They look lifeless. I barely notice. I'm too busy listening to the shuffle of the kids in every homeroom moving into their seats in the auditorium.

The Student Council President, who waits with me, moves his note cards to the bottom of the stack, one by one, without even looking at them. I start going through my own cards again, but I can't concentrate. I assume Mom and Dad are seated in the front row with the other parents. Is Emma with them?

Mom and Dad never asked how or why the envelope addressed to her disappeared from the dresser. I'm not about to ask questions.

If Emma shows up today, she'll tell them I came by, but I'm pretty sure she'll have a class or an appointment or a dead battery or some other excuse. Her loss.

It's an awful thing to admit, but I want to know how close Bri and Azita were. Did they do more than kiss? Did they go all the way? Bri slept with Emma at the end of his senior year. I found a pack of condoms in the back of his desk, and if he bought them, I'm pretty sure he used them.

I've never gotten any further than kissing. Diego's kiss last night was magical, but Rob's kisses at the party were intense and scary. So why does Rob pop into my brain as often as Diego?

I'm so busy thinking about those two that I almost jump when I hear, "Now Sandee Mason will speak about her brother, Brian. Many of you will remember him as a scholar athlete who worked on Student Council, excelled at track, and was on the Honor Roll seven out of eight semesters. He graduated last spring and wanted to serve in the military before going to college, but he never made it back to fulfill that dream. Sandee?"

I come out from behind the curtain with my sweat-rimmed notes in hand. I set them on the podium, pull down my new metallic black sweater, turn on the PowerPoint and say, "Brian Mason was my older brother, but I think everybody here already knows that. Sometimes he treated me like a kid sister, but other times he'd come into my room and tell me about high school—about this school—where we are right now and where he used to be. He might have sat where you're sitting today."

Everybody looks at me. Mom's smiling even though her chin trembles.

I need a deep breath before I can say, "Sometimes it's hard to believe he's never coming back."

"Shut up," someone yells from the back row.

Mr. Hawkins stands up and peers at the kids in his homeroom. "Who said that?"

"He dissed me," Rob yells and points to a guy the kids call Bruiser. "Sorry, Sandee. Go for it," he calls across the entire audience in his stage manager voice.

"Thanks, Rob," I say into the mike. I tell the audience, "Rob was one of Bri's good friends, and they hung out at our house on Saturdays when they were in middle school. I know Rob misses Bri as much as my family does. Rob was almost a member of the family a few years back."

"Drama fag!" a hoarse voice coughs out. The rude kids usually do that to subs. Everyone hears it because I hear it from the front of the stage.

"Shut up, asshole," Rob screams, lunging towards Bruiser, who looks a little like the boy playing Jud. Rob's raging, like he did at the Saturday workday. He hurls himself over his chair and into Bruiser's row.

Bruiser and his buddy slip behind a wall of muscle-bound losers who pump their fists and take up the chant. Kids from other homerooms join them, and Rob totally doesn't deserve that. Nobody does. The whole auditorium pulsates with "Fag, fag, drama fag."

I know we have gay kids in drama, but the school has a zero tolerance policy on name-calling. Besides, Rob's not gay, and everybody knows it. Is that why he's so mad? His face is beet red, and I can see the white knuckles on his fists all the way up onstage.

Mr. Hawkins shoves his way through the losers and grabs Bruiser and his buddy, who keep pumping their fists like this is some huge victory. An assistant principal charges in to help. Everybody's chanting now, and nobody's listening to me.

Dr. Henderson rushes up from the front row and grabs my mike. "Settle down, everyone. Just settle down," he says over and over.

Mr. Hawkins and the assistant principal haul Bruiser and Rob out of the auditorium. At the same time, Dr. Henderson says, "Eyes up here," to the whole student body. "Now!"

The kids ignore him. Even after the auditorium door slams, everybody's rehashing what happened. Some of the teachers move into the aisles. I grip the edges of the podium. Mom is clutching Dad's arm.

"Disruptions of this kind will not be tolerated anywhere on this campus. That includes assemblies, the lunchroom, and the sports fields. If you understand, stop talking to your neighbor and raise your hand," Dr. Henderson says.

A few people do. Then about a quarter of them catch on. I see a teacher listing the names of those ignoring him as more and more hands go up. Mine does too.

"Stand up if you understand," Dr. Henderson says when 75 percent of the kids have their hands up. I'm already standing, so I look out as the cheerleaders and jocks, the honor roll members, the geeks and the band and their friends all stand up. The quiet ones and the wannabes follow them. Finally, the troublemakers stand up, though a number of them keep their arms folded over their chests or stuffed in their pockets.

"Unless you want detention and a call to your parents, you are to open your minds instead of your mouths and keep your attention on the program. Miss Mason, are you ready to continue?"

Nobody's ever called me Miss Mason before. My stomach flutters, but no one can tell as I say, "Thank you, Dr. Henderson," in a silky-smooth voice.

Being Miss Mason gives me dignity. Bri would be proud.

The PowerPoint is frozen on the last slide, which says, "Figuring out who you are is the whole point of the human experience." I don't know whether to start it again or leave it alone.

I look at my notes. They no longer make sense, but Dr. Henderson hands me the mike, and I have to talk. My speech is about serving our country, but everybody here is too wrapped up in their own worlds and the fight Bruiser provoked to think about being of service.

Tessa's comparison between being in a show and being in the military flashes through my mind. So does Ms. Marron's mantra about reaching your audience when you give a speech.

"Well, the PowerPoint is done, and I'm not sure how much you saw of it," I say to identify a problem we all share. "Maybe I can post it on the school's website, if that's okay with Dr. Henderson."

"That's a fine idea, Sandee," he says, and I catch my parents nodding out of the corner of my eyes.

"I hope you don't mind looking at this last slide for a while. I took it off of the bulletin board over Bri's desk. The message *Figuring out who you are is the whole point of the human experience* has more meaning for me all of the time.

"When you're in the Army, you don't get to blurt out like Bruiser just did. You don't have time for stuff like name-calling and false accusations. In the Army, lives are at stake. My dad taught me that. He served in the Army during the first Iraq War.

"Bri believed in serving his country. Rob believes in helping the school put on shows. Both of them want to help others. I have friends who sing and dance and help out any way they can. Drama people want to build something up instead of tearing it down the way those guys just did.

"Sometimes I ask myself, 'What would Brian want you to do?' It's not like asking 'What would Jesus do?' because Bri isn't perfect—wasn't," I correct myself. There isn't a sound in the house now. I take a deep breath so my voice won't quiver.

"Bri was a good, smart kid, and he didn't deserve to die. If he were here today, I hope he'd say, 'I'm sorry I left you.' He'd probably say he was trying to do the right thing. I used to believe that. Now I'm not always sure.

"If you knew Bri, make up your own mind about whether or not his time in Afghanistan was worth it. People should always make up their own minds and stand up for what they believe in, and I think Rob was doing exactly that when he told the guy who dissed him to shut up. That makes him a kind of hero. I guess all kinds of things can make a person a hero, but the people who die when they become heroes, the people who die serving their country, are exceptional."

Dr. Henderson takes the mike from me and says, "Thank you, Sandee." He holds the curtain open in the center, which tells me I'm done. "Because of our interruption earlier, we're short on time," I hear him say when I'm behind the curtain with the ghost light and our set. "I know Tessa Kwan hasn't read from the journal she's keeping for her sister. Student Council hasn't read their Honor Roll of San Ramos High School students who died in the War on Terror. Please share those with my secretary, and we'll get them on the website.

"Since this is a Wednesday, I need to dismiss B-lunch people to fourth period and A-lunch people to the cafeteria."

Then, that's it. The assembly is over.

At lunch I hunt for Rob. I can't wait to tell him I told the whole student body he's a hero.

He's not in the lunch line or at the drama table. Nicole's there, though, and when I ask her if she knows where Rob is, she leans in and says, "He told Jenn he isn't going to put up with all the crap in this place and headed for the parking lot. I hope he calms down before rehearsal."

"Me too."

"I love what you said about Bri, but you were wrong about one thing: Rob's no hero."

"You don't think it was heroic of him to defend the drama kids?"

"I think heroes have more self-control, but he's not my problem anymore. I'm no longer his girlfriend."

Jenn straddles the bench as Nicole opens her water bottle. Jenn pulls out the Tupperware that holds today's salad and says, "Cool speech, Sandee."

"Thanks." I turn back to Nicole and ask, "Did you actually see him leave campus?"

"He got in his Honda and drove away."

"Who left campus?" Jenn asks. Does she have any clue that she's interrupting something important?

"I'll see you at rehearsal, okay?" I tell Nicole. I need to check the parking lot and see if he's back. I go up and down the rows, but his Honda is gone. What is he thinking? We have a closed campus. What if the police catch him?

I pull out my iPhone. If I can get him to come back before lunch is over, maybe he won't be expelled.

As soon as he says, "Hellooooo," I can tell he's been drinking.

"Where are you?"

"Who wants to know?"

"I want to know. It's Sandee, in case your vision's so blurry you can't read your screen. What are you doing, Rob?"

"Celebratin."

"What are you celebrating?"

"Your assembly. Your brother. Graduation. Only three months until graduation. I swear to God a diploma is a license to go out in the world and get yourself killed."

"What are you talking about? Bri didn't want to die. Can you hear how crazy you sound?" I sling my backpack over one shoulder. "Tell me where you are, and I'll come and get you."

"No way." Frogs croak in the background.

"You're at the creek behind our house, right?"

"Wrong. Try again."

That means he wants to be rescued. At least I hope he does. Where else does the creek run? By the Presbyterian church. Behind the library. Underneath the freeway. Out on Valley Road. "Just tell me, Rob. Where are you?"

"You worry too much, Sandee. Everything will be fine."

"Not if you walked off campus without a note. How can you let everyone down like this?"

"Everyone?"

"We can't do the show if you're suspended, dork-head." I hear nothing but Rob's breathing on the other end. Even the frogs are silent.

"I'll be back for rehearsal, and I'll be sober enough. No one's going to suspect anything unless you open your stupid mouth."

"Let me come and walk you home."

"Don't be absurd. When I'm ready to go, I'll drive myself."

"You want your own DUI?"

"I told you once before. I'm way smarter than Nicole." There's a hard edge in his voice.

"So be smart. Let me come and get you. Where are you?"

"Where do you think I'd be?"

"You're at Osage Park where you and Bri used to play Little League, aren't you?" His silence confirms it. "Stay there." I hear the low rumble of the BART bus coming down San Ramos Boulevard.

I clutch my phone and race towards the bus with my backpack thumping behind me. Osage Park is a fifteen-minute walk or a three-minute ride. I barely have time to catch my breath before I hop off.

I walk across the close-cropped grass and scan the aluminum bleachers.

Rob sits with his legs spread wide, on the bleachers facing left field. He's slumped against the thin, metal edge of the bench behind him. He drops an empty bottle, and it clatters against one that's already on the ground.

"Brian, guide me," I whisper as I head across the field. "Rob is in big trouble, and I'm not sure how to help."

CHAPTER THIRTY-NINE

SOMETIMES THE BEST THING a friend can do is listen. I learned that working on my last scene for drama class, but what are you supposed to do if the scene is real and the "character" is a drunk senior who gets to tell you what to do during rehearsal?

Scenes end, but real life keeps going. Ms. G told us once that characters drink so they can say things they wouldn't say if they were sober. So what is Rob afraid to say?

As soon as I'm in earshot, Rob starts in about the stupid jock that dissed him and how lame everybody's gotten and how grateful he'll be when he graduates.

He finally stops to breathe and I ask, "What happened after Hawkins hauled you out?" I look out on the field where Bri and he played Saturday-morning Little League.

"Henderson wasn't there, so Wong yelled at us about rudeness and selfishness and a bunch of other crap."

"And?" I ask when his eyes glaze over.

"We're on lunch detention and Saturday school, and I'm banned from all co-curricular activities until I'm done."

"But that means—"

Rob goes right on as if I haven't spoken. "I told her it was crappy timing, and I asked if I could start it after the show closed." I close my eyes, knowing what he'll say next. "She said no, of course, so now I have to convince Ms. G to override her." He takes another swig of beer.

I can't believe him. "Put that thing down. You're in enough trouble." He ignores me and drinks so long that beer dribbles down his chin. "What about all the people who are counting on you?"

"I doan wanna think about it."

"Give me the bottle." He dangles it over his head, but I'm quick enough to grab it. The little bit that's left splashes on both of us. He starts to laugh.

"What's so funny?" I ask.

"You fighting me. Silly girl. Don't turn this into *The Days of Wine and Roses*."

I slide the bottle out of his grip. He barely notices. "Time to go home. We've got rehearsal in a few hours."

I hope his mom will write him a note so he doesn't get more detention for cutting. Mine too. I have Ms. Brunskill for PE. She turns in anyone who isn't standing in the right place when she gets outside with her roll book.

"Give me your keys," I say, pouring his beer on the ground.

He hands them over. Maybe he's forgotten that I won't get my license until next week. Maybe he doesn't care because he says, "You're the best, Sandee," and throws a limp arm around my neck. His breath reeks.

I pour him into the passenger seat, go around, and sit in the driver's seat. I put the key in the ignition, adjust the mirrors, and back carefully out of the parking space. I shift into drive. This is easy, even though I've only driven his Honda once.

"You feel any better?" I ask two minutes later as I turn onto Garretson Drive.

No answer. His head is tipped back, and his mouth hangs open. A minute later, his snores are louder than my dad's. I turn right on Brookside. At Valley Drive, I signal for another right, but when I look in my rearview mirror, I see a flashing strip of lights on top of a black-and-white car.

My heart beats against the lining of my stomach. I reach over and shake Rob. He snores louder.

An officer with bushy eyebrows and a determined look pounds on my window. I push the button, but it won't go down. I've turned off the engine.

He signals that I need to lower the window, and as soon as I do he says, "License and registration, please?" in an all-business voice that's closer to tenor than bass.

We role-played this situation in Driver's Ed. When I played the cop, I knew who was blowing me off and who was truly sorry. Be polite and don't argue, I tell myself.

I reach past Rob, search his glove box, and hand the registration to the officer, who asks, "Are you Susan Cooper?"

"No."

"Your mother?" He peers in at me, and I know he's waiting for me to trip up, but I'm completely in control. "No. She's his mother." I gesture towards Rob. "He didn't feel good, so I'm driving him home."

"Is he inebriated?"

I want to protect Rob, so I say, "He's not driving, Officer." I hope he doesn't think I'm a smart-ass.

"May I see your license please?" I fish around in my backpack, although I have no license in it. "Well?"

Slowly I pull out my wallet. I open it up, pull up my student body card, my library card, and finally say, "What did I do?"

He knows I'm stalling. I can see it in his face. "Your license?" he says again, holding out his hand.

If he sees my permit, I'm busted. I won't get a license until I'm eighteen.

No way that's happening. "Um. Give me a minute." I open the glove box again, while Rob snores. The officer flips a switch on the transmitter he wears on his shoulder and calls for backup.

My heart pounds against my chest. "You don't need backup. This is my license." He glances at it and rolls his eyes. "I know it's only a permit, but look at my birthday. I'll be sixteen in six days. I know how to drive."

"But you're not a licensed driver, are you?"

"Rob is sick. He needs a ride. His mom's at work, so there's no one to pick him up." I can't stop the flood of excuses. "Please, sir, let me get him home."

This must be how Rob felt when Bruiser called him a fag. He reacted like a caged animal being poked with a stick, but the penalty for driving without a license is way worse than getting kicked out of an assembly. He told me he got two weeks. I'll get two years. I'll be stuck bumming rides until I'm eighteen. Ms. G will have to call the cues because we can't stage-manage from juvenile hall, and that's where we'll both be when the curtain goes up. What will my parents think? What about college? Am I going to Pine Mountain with Nicole?

The officer takes my permit and goes back to his car. I'll probably never see it again. I punch Rob in the arm. "Will you wake up?" His snore grows louder. "Rob, we are in deep trouble. I need your help."

Rob says, "Mmmfffhhh," and bats my hand away. The red lights keep rotating behind us.

"He'll have to sleep it off, Miss Mason, and he'll be doing it at juvenile hall unless he's over eighteen," the officer says.

"You don't understand. He's seventeen, and he got drunk because he lost his best friend. Didn't you ever do something wrong when you were his age?"

He doesn't answer. Instead, he gets back into his car and punches something into his computer. A moment later he asks, "Is this your brother, Rob?"

"What?"

"Is he your brother?"

"My brother. . . " My voice warbles as I say it. "My brother died in the war in Afghanistan."

"Your permit says you're Sandee Mason."

"Right."

"Well, someone named Rob Mason, who matches this boy's description, picked you up at the BART station last Thursday night according to your record. The report says there was a lot of teenage defiance, but they let you go with a warning. Is that right?"

"Almost. He's not. . ." I can't do this. I can't lie to cover for him. I know I promised I wouldn't tell, but I owe it to Bri to keep his record clean.

A second police car pulls up and the officer who bounds out says, "Hey, Miller. Whatcha got?"

"Inebriation and underage driving."

The new officer has blue eyes and a face full of freckles. He takes off his sunglasses and looks me over thoroughly before he asks, "Have you had anything to drink today?"

I shake my head.

"What about your friend?"

"You can find out if he's been drinking with one of your DUI tests." I can't believe myself, but his being on the record as Rob Mason makes me want revenge.

The new officer, Gorman, leans into my face and says, "Don't get smart with me, young lady."

"Sorry, but I don't want to answer for him."

"Loyalty. That's rare. You know you're driving his car with no license, right?"

"I don't mean to be disrespectful, Officer, but would it have been better to let him drive himself?"

"Unlock the passenger door," Officer Gorman says, ignoring my question.

I push the button and say, "Door unlocked," as if I'm responding to a stage manager's cue, but this isn't a play or a musical, and the officers from the sheriff's department are pulling the stage manager of *Oklahoma!* out of his mom's car, which I just drove without a license.

My dad says when you want to know something you have to ask, so I say, "Why did you stop me?" I look old enough to drive, so they need probable cause.

"Your taillight is broken."

"All this because of a broken taillight?"

"It was." That sprawling lump of snores in the passenger seat compounds it. "Is he your boyfriend?"

I shake my head. Nicole's right. Who'd want this drunken mess for a boyfriend?

Miller pulls him out and flattens him against his mom's car while Gorman clicks the cuffs around his wrists. He wakes up enough to ask, "What's up?"

"You're being arrested, Rob," Gorman says. "That's your name, isn't it? You're Mrs. Cooper's son, Robert, and this is her car that you've let your unlicensed friend drive, right? You're going to juvenile hall, and we'll tow your car unless the registered owner comes and picks it up."

Rob says, "Who are you guys and where did you get the costumes?" Then he throws up; his mom's Honda and the ground next to it stink of barf and booze.

Miller turns to me and says, "Get out and sit on the curb, little lady." I don't like sitting on the cold cement, but at least he doesn't put me in handcuffs or force me to sit next to Rob.

I don't know if Rob will get to keep his license. He wasn't driving drunk, so he might, and it doesn't seem fair that I may lose my permit when I was only trying to help.

Gorman eases Rob into the back seat of his police car, gets in the front, and drives away. I'm left alone with Miller, who comes towards me and says, "I have to handcuff you right now for my own safety. Do you understand?" I don't answer. "Do you understand?" he shouts.

"I get it," I shout back. This is so much more unfair than what happened to Rob in the assembly. If Bruiser hadn't started his stupid chant, none of this would have happened.

"Turn around and put your hands behind your back." I wipe the tears away before I turn around, but it doesn't help. I can't stop crying as I hear the metal cuffs click together. The steel is cold around my wrists. "Well, young lady, what do you think of the consequences of breaking the law?"

"I don't like them, but I'm still glad I didn't let Rob get behind the wheel," I say through my tears.

"What if you scraped the side of a car or hit a child in a crosswalk?" I can't look at him, much less speak. "Well, little lady?"

"Nothing happened. Why can't you give me credit for doing something right?"

He doesn't answer. Instead he goes back to his car. A minute later he's back. "Do you have your phone on you?"

"In my pocket." I can't even reach for it. A car drives by, and I can feel the driver's eyes on me.

He goes into my contacts and says, "I'm calling 'Dad,' okay?" I stare at my shoes. "You don't have to say anything. I'll talk to him."

"No. I'll talk." I can imagine Dad reading my name and saying, "We're so proud of your speech, Sandee," right before he hears, "This isn't Sandee; it's Officer Gorman of the San Ramos Police Department."

I'm still in handcuffs, so he puts the phone to my ear. I hear, "You have reached Grayco Insurance. We're out of the office, but if you leave your name and number, someone will get back to you. If this is an emergency, please call my secretary, Angie Johnson, at 555-1324."

He only puts that impersonal message on his cell when he and his secretary are both out of the office. "Dad, it's Sandee. It's kind of an emergency. I need to talk to you. Call me!"

Officer Miller scrolls down and says, "I'm looking for Mom, okay?" He holds the phone up to my ear again, but Mom's phone also goes to her messages after the second ring. "We have to release you to the custody of a responsible adult," Officer Miller says.

It takes me about ten seconds to realize I'll have to call Ms. G. We have three hours until our final dress rehearsal, and the stage manager is on his way to jail.

CHAPTER FORTY

TEN MINUTES LATER, MS. G hops out of her car and heads towards me, but Miller blocks her. They both stand there with their arms folded as he explains that Rob is drunk and using a false name. "He's on his way to juvenile hall right now," Officer Miller says.

"Are you arresting Sandee too?" My insides shake.

"It's illegal to drive without a license, but we'll talk to her parents before we decide whether we're charging her. She's got no priors other than an argument at BART last weekend, and she was trying to keep a drunk off the road, so we might let her off with a ticket and a fine." Whatever I get, it beats sleeping in a six-by-eight cell. "In the meantime she's either in your custody or she follows Rob to juvenile hall until her parents can pick her up."

Acid lines my stomach. I'd wrap my arms around it, but I'm still in handcuffs.

"You've called the Masons?" Ms. G asks.

"Neither one answered."

The corners of her lips turn up slightly as she says, "Sandee will be at the San Ramos High Theater until after 10:30 tonight. When the show's over, we'll try her parents again. Now, what's this business about Rob using an alias?"

"Rob Mason is the name in our records for a boy matching his description who tried to pick up Sandee at BART last Friday."

Ms. G looks pale. "Rob knows better than to use an alias. Sandee's brother, Brian Mason, was killed in Afghanistan. Rob's last name is Cooper." She sits on the curb next to me and asks, "What's going on, Sandee?"

I don't know where to start. "The BART Police were acting like . . . well, they made some stupid assumptions and called Rob my brother. I'm not sure if he said it or they did, but he didn't deny it when he heard it."

Even though I'm telling her facts, I'm not sure I'm telling the whole truth. Rob's my friend, and if he's developing a drinking problem, then maybe I need to say something before it gets any worse, but I don't want to be a snitch. My family taught me to be honest, but they also taught me to be loyal, and I'm not sure what to do. What would Nicole or Tessa or Diego do? What would Bri do?

A quiet voice outside my head says, "Trust your instincts, Sandee—even when the choices get hard."

Tears roll down my face. I can't even reach up to wipe them away. Bri's around. I'm sure of it.

"Can you tell me why you were driving Rob's car?"

"He got drunk. I think it's because he misses Bri, or maybe it was my speech, or maybe it was Bruiser. I wanted to get him home and sobered up before rehearsal."

Ms. G says, "Officer, if you'll take the handcuffs off this young lady, I'll keep an eye on her until her parents pick her up at the theater, and I promise she'll be busy all evening."

He slips his key into the lock on the handcuffs and says, "You stay with your drama teacher until your folks pick you up. You understand? If you try to run or cause any more trouble, I can guarantee you'll be charged."

"Yes, sir."

"Are you performing in that show tonight?" he asks while I rub my wrists. My eyes fill with tears again. I don't know if I'm crying over having no role, Rob going to jail, Brian being dead, or all of them. I wipe my eyes with my newly freed hands. "No sir," I say when I can talk. "I'll be backstage, guarding props."

Ms. G surprises me when she puts an arm around me and walks me to her Saturn. As we drive away, she says, "You know I'll have to talk to your parents."

I don't trust my voice, so I nod. As she drives me back to the auditorium, I stare down the streets Diego and I walk together so often. I haven't seen him since the end of the assembly when he came up and said, "You rock, Sandee. Bri would be proud."

"Is there anything you want to tell me before I speak with your parents? I'm sure there's more to this story than I just heard."

I like Ms. G, but she's a teacher. I have no idea if she ever had a brother, much less lost one. She knows about characters, but real people are another matter. I don't think I have anything to say until I hear myself ask, "Do you know how much drinking some of the drama kids do?"

"On campus?" she asks as she stops at a red light.

"Don't you care about us when we're not on campus?"

She takes her eyes off the road, and I squirm when she looks at me.

"Of course I care," she says as the light changes. "I know the drama kids did a lot of partying last year, but I thought the ringleaders graduated. Are you telling me they're still getting together to party every Friday night?"

"Some are." I know she's a teacher, and she's not going to take sides, so I say, "Look, I know you've worked with Rob a long time, so maybe you can't see it, but I think he drinks every day, and last night, he might have been drinking in the booth. I don't know how to help him." She stares out the windshield so long that I finally ask, "Did you hear what I said?"

"I don't have a lot of firsthand experience with alcohol or drugs, but I think you helped him more than you know today. As soon as we get back to the theater, I'll call his mom and tell her where the car is and why you have the keys. Then I'm going to call your parents and tell them that you're as much of a hero as your brother. You may have saved Rob's life today. I'm very proud of you, Sandee. You have empathy for others. That's rare in someone your age."

I can't believe I tear up again. She hands me a Kleenex, and I blow my nose.

"I'm sorry you haven't gotten more recognition for that. It's a real talent, but it's certainly not your only one." As she pulls into the school parking lot she says, "Right now I could really use your help getting things ready backstage, okay?"

"Absolutely." It's nice to be trusted.

CHAPTER 43

WHEN WE GET TO the theater, I'm ashamed to go in. Ms. G says, "I thought you told me you didn't do anything wrong?"

"True, but being in handcuffs made me feel . . . I don't know. I'm sick of no one believing me."

"I believe you, and I need your help to get this place ready. Could you start by making sure there's no trash under the seats?"

Typical ASM job. Ms. G sits in the front row and calls Rob's mom. As I work my way up and down the rows, I hear her say, "You need to pick up your car before the police tow it away."

Mrs. Cooper must ask why because Ms. G explains what happened. Then there's a long pause before she says, "It's going to be okay," and "I don't think he did it to hurt you."

Rob's mom must feel guiltier than I do. She hates being a single parent. I hate the fact that Bri isn't coming home. Do both of our losses trigger guilt because it's too late to change the past?

This isn't her fault. It isn't mine, either. Without Rob here, I'll probably have twice as much work to do.

The minute Ms. G gets off the phone, she says, "Sandee, could you sweep the stage while I try your dad again?"

He doesn't answer—again—so I say, "I'll check the costume room, too, and hang up anything that's out of place."

"That's what I like to hear," she says even though she's texting someone.

The costume room looks neat and orderly. If a person knew when it would be like this, he could easily sneak in and hide guns, but right now, it's so quiet I can hear the overhead fluorescents hum. I sneak a look behind the shoes. No new guns have appeared. If anything's missing, it's not obvious. I go back upstairs, and the minute I reappear onstage Ms. G asks, "Do you remember how to check the lights?"

"Absolutely. I'm on it."

Tessa, who has come in to add pillows to Aunt Eller's rocking chair and clothes to the laundry line says, "You sound like a TV detective when you say that, Sandee."

Is she nuts? I want to stay as far from the police as I can after this afternoon.

When I finish testing the lights, I go backstage, and Tessa says, "You did a really good job today, going on after Rob and Bruiser and his friend got hauled out." I'm about to ask if she knows that Rob walked off campus and got drunk when she says, "I wondered if you'd be interested in talking to some of our groups about the legacy that a soldier leaves."

"Sure. Wait a minute. What are you talking about?"

"Once a month, the Blue Star Moms support group hosts a big meeting in Oakland. We look for a speaker who can give us a message of hope. I think you've already got the speech, and we have an opening for a speaker in July. I know it's four months away, but are you interested?"

My heart pounds louder than drums at a concert. "Sure. Why not?"

"That's great. It's a huge gathering, but they have TVs so everyone can see, and of course, you'll have a mike. We usually pay an honorarium."

"What's that?" I ask as I pick up stray scraps of lighting gel that someone swept into a backstage corner.

"It's money. Cash. We paid $250 last month."

"Are you kidding me?"

"Do I sound like I'm kidding?"

I throw my arms around her. "That's awesome! When and where?"

"I'll be in touch. You and I have a lot in common, and I think we're going to be friends long after this show is over."

"I'm sorry you didn't get to read from your journal during the assembly," I say.

"I just hope I get to share it with her when she wakes up. I'm doing it for her."

She goes back to work. I sit down by the props cabinet and text Mom and Dad. "I have to talk to you. You're going to get a call from Ms. G or the police. It sounds worse than it is. I tried to rescue Rob by driving him home. He was drunk. I was pulled over for a broken taillight—not bad driving." I almost click send, but there's more, and if I don't say it now, I'll lose my courage.

"Something's wrong with Rob," I type. "He can't stop drinking, and I don't know how to help him. Also, if you saw the PowerPoint, you know I looked through Bri's footlocker without your permission. I saw his note to Emma and delivered it. I'm trying to be responsible. I hope you don't get mad because I took some initiative. I love you both and we'll get through this together."

I hit send at the same moment Ms. G asks, "Are the props ready?" Jenn and Diego stand by the empty props table. If they came together, I'll . . . I'll live with it, I guess, but as I hear Jenn ask, "Where are they? Where's Sandee?" I realize she's only into herself right now.

"I was just about to set out the props for the first act. Why aren't you two downstairs getting dressed?"

"We want to check our props first. No biggie."

"We can come back," Diego adds, and he winks at me behind Jenn's back.

"Good plan."

Jenn doesn't pay any attention to me, which probably means the news of Rob's arrest hasn't reached Facebook yet. If she knew, she'd have to share.

Instead, she says, "I'm going downstairs to turn myself into a prairie chick." Diego stays behind, staring at the outline for his knife on the props table.

"Something wrong?" I ask.

"You tell me. Why did you cut this afternoon?" He won't look at me. "Were you doing an interview for the school paper or something?"

I laugh, and he looks more puzzled than ever. "Believe it or not, I was trying to save our stage manager—the one who got hauled out of the assembly earlier today."

I tell him what Nicole said about Rob storming out of the office, heading for the parking lot, and taking off. I explain about our phone call, his slurred voice, and how I remembered the creek by the park. "I didn't know what to do, but no one else can run the show, so I tried to talk him into coming back before sixth period. When I saw he was too wasted to be on campus or drive, I—"

"You didn't."

"Would it have been better for me to let him drive drunk?"

Diego says exactly the same thing as the police. "Did you think about calling his parents? Or maybe a licensed driver?"

"I had too much adrenaline surging through me to think of anything but saving Rob and the show. I know I'm no star, but I thought saving Rob would save the show. I actually thought I was doing a Sandee Special. Remember those?"

Diego takes me in his arms and holds me close. When my sobs stop, he says, "What you did was gutsy. You're my girl, and I'll always stand by you."

"Oh, Diego," I say, and the tears well up again.

"What's wrong now?"

I shake my head. He has done nothing wrong. Nothing at all.

"Doncha wanna be my womern?" he asks in his best Cord Elam voice.

I start to laugh. He's clowning around again, but he called me a "womern," and asked me to be his "womern." No one has ever called me a woman before.

I laugh harder, and he says, "Womern, if you cain't stop laughing, I'm gonna kiss ya." He puts his arms around me. I'm laughing and crying, and this is not at all how I once imagined becoming Diego's girlfriend. His lips touch mine. A moment later, our mouths melt together. All the pressures, fears, hopes, and disappointments of the last twenty-four hours and the last nine weeks melt into that long, joyous kiss.

We aren't Clark Gable and Vivian Leigh or Richard Gere and Julia Roberts or any other classic couple. We aren't even the leads in *Oklahoma!* We are ourselves, in the roles we are supposed to play at this exact moment in our lives, and when we pull away, I think I hear Bri say, "Way to go, Sandee. You know how to pick 'em."

I want to ask Diego if he heard it too, but I refuse to spoil the moment for either one of us. Tessa comes by with the plants for Aunt Eller's porch and says, "You two an item now?"

"Who warnts to know?" Diego asks. All three of us burst out laughing.

Once the cast and the orchestra sign in, Ms. G finds me in the dressing room, pinning a side seam in Jenn's skirt. She says, "Sandee, I need to see you in the house," and she sounds firm.

"I hope it's not about the police."

"The police?" Tessa asks.

Diego hears her through the curtain and says, "Meet me backstage and I'll tell you everything." I trust him to get it right.

When I show up in the house, Ms. G says, "The police got ahold of your parents. They misunderstood and were on their way to Martinez to bail you out when they called to let me know you wouldn't be at the show. Imagine their relief when I told them you were in the theater getting ready for opening night. They said they'll be right over, but I asked them to wait until the show was over to see you."

"Why?"

"You'll find out soon. In the meantime, will you run the cues with the follow-spot operators? I don't have time to do it."

I go to the booth and read the cues out of the prompt book and wonder whether the revolvers are safe backstage and whether Rob is safe at juvenile hall.

An hour before the final dress rehearsal starts, we gather on the apron. "Before I give notes from last night," Ms. G says, "I want to tell you that I've overheard students and faculty saying wonderful things about your presentation this morning, Sandee. You showed confidence and composure when things got out of hand. Your preparation paid off."

"Look at her. She's beaming," the actor playing Curley says. "Way to go, Sanders."

Diego takes my hand.

Ms. G holds up her hand to stop the chatter. "If you were at the assembly, you saw a fight break out. Our stage manager, Rob Cooper, was involved, and I know many of you heard he walked out of the office at lunch and left campus."

"I heard he got drunk," an actor in Levi's and a checked shirt says.

"He's always drunk these days," one of the girls from the chorus adds, shaking her head in disgust.

"I heard he mouthed off to an officer and got arrested," the boy who plays Jud tells us. "When did he get so stupid?"

Ms. G holds up her hand again. "The bottom line is that he won't be here to stage manage our final dress rehearsal, so I'm asking our assistant stage manager, Sandee Mason, to take over. Sandee, you've shown us how much you're capable of backstage, and today we learned what a good speaker you are. Tonight we need you to run the show. I'm asking Tessa to keep an eye on the props because you're replacing Rob as our stage manager."

Diego beams at me. "Way to go, Sandee."

"Awesome!" Tessa says, high-fiving me.

"Girls rock!" Nicole shouts from across the room.

For the third time, Ms. G holds up her hand. "I want you to know that Sandee's the youngest stage manager we've ever had. She has shown a remarkable ability to resolve problems and a great deal of moral fiber—especially in the last twenty-four hours. I expect everyone to give her your complete and full cooperation. Now, we're going to take thirty minutes so Sandee can run the cues with all lighting technicians and stagehands. Use the time to run your own cues and lines, get into character, vocalize, and double-check anything you need to. We're going to have an audience tonight."

"Not the people from Pine Mountain College." Jenn looks like she's about to cry.

"No, Jenn. A local reporter attended today's assembly. She was particularly impressed by Sandee's speech. She called her 'a composed and talented young woman,' and asked to attend our show before she writes her article. Let's show her just how much talent we have on this campus, okay?"

This time the ensemble bursts into applause.

I breathe deeply, taking in the fact that a local reporter called me "a composed and talented young woman." Then I belt out the words, "One hour to curtain." Actors pair up to run lines, and the techies go to their stations.

Ms. G comes over and hands me the keys and a headset. All she says is, "Some of the headsets are still locked in the lighting booth. Please get them so we can get started," but her eyes say volumes more.

"Absolutely." I start running the cues in my head. "House lights, ready; house lights, go. Curtain warmers, ready; curtain warmers, go."

EPILOGUE

THE FIRST WEEK IN June, Pine Mountain College held its auditions. Nicole got two supporting roles, one in *Hairspray* and one in *Guys and Dolls*. She has been beaming ever since rehearsals started.

I hope she won't be too hard to live with in the fall—if she comes back. Maybe she'll get her GED and stay at Pine Mountain until her probation ends.

Jenn also auditioned. The directors told her she showed great promise. She's in the *Hairspray* chorus, where she'll sing and dance behind a 200-pound college girl playing the lead. Nicole says they picked the show for that girl. I love it.

Jenn's collecting props for *Guys and Dolls*. She texted me for help after raiding her parents' props room and coming up with less than half of what she needs, so I'm a props advisor for Pine Mountain College's Summerfest. How awesome is that?

Diego's band started getting gigs for parties—okay, kid's birthday parties, but you have to start somewhere. He plans to try out for the next musical. I'll try out with him, and I'll be wearing his ring when I do. Maybe this sounds corny, but I love having a boyfriend.

I've started working two days a week after school at Generation to Generation. It pays, but that's not why I'm doing it. Mom wants to spend more time with me. Like Jenn and Diego, she and I have to start somewhere if we're going to get our relationship back. Besides, I might find some real treasures while I'm unpacking boxes.

Mom and Dad understood about my driving Rob's car. So did the police, once they had all the facts. Rob's mom pleaded with them not to penalize me for saving her son from driving drunk.

My birthday was the Monday after opening weekend. Dad picked me up right after school and took me to the DMV. I passed my driver's test with a 91 percent. Woo-hoo!

So now I drive Dad to his office unless he has appointments in the field, and then I take the car to school. Sometimes I give Diego and Jenn rides home.

When I go down the hall past Bri's room, I whisper, "I'm getting on with my life."

Sometimes I hear him say, "You go, girl." Unless I imagine it. I never completely figured out where his voice comes from, but I feel his support, even though I can't prove it's there.

When Mom and I get home from Generation to Generation one afternoon, I find a letter from Rob in the mailbox.

Hi Sandee,

Old fashioned letters suck, but that's all you can send from New Hope.

Believe it or not, I want to thank you for trying to take me home. My lawyer said you didn't get busted. WTG! You didn't deserve to wind up in jail because of me. I guess you know they got me for being drunk in public, and the judge sent me to rehab. Jenn probably put it on Facebook.

I honestly don't know whether I drink too much or not. Whenever I say that in an AA meeting, the chair tells me to close my mouth and open my ears. I know you never expected me to say this, but it's kind of nice having someone else in charge.

Ever since Bri disappeared, I had a terrible feeling that he wasn't coming back. I wanted to be there for you when you got the news because you're his kid sister, and I've known you forever, but you didn't need me. You did fine on your own. Again. I wish I'd told you that you had it all together.

You do, you know. You used to be Bri's little sister, but you're so much more now. If he were here, Bri would agree, and if you weren't his sister, he'd say, "Why don't you go out with her, Rob?"

Any interest?

It can't hurt to try.

One more thing I have to tell you. You were partly right when you thought someone was trying to sabotage the show. Somebody was out to make you look bad because you were so damned competent. He never thought about what it would do to the show because he knew he could make the guns reappear whenever he wanted to.

He still doesn't know how the auditorium's security cameras missed him, but he's grateful now and a lot more humble than he was when he thought he was God's gift to drama.

I hope you and I can start over again after I get out of here. You're a cool chick, Sandee, whether you know it or not. For what it's worth, Bri would want you to believe in yourself.

Write back if you want to. It looks like I'm going to be here for longer than I thought. Maybe I can start at Pine Mountain in January.

Rob

I can't write back. Not right now. I'm meeting Diego for coffee in ten minutes. "See you later," I call as I open the door.

Mom sticks her head through the kitchen door and says, "Take your cell."

"We're proud of you, honey," Dad calls out. That's what they both used to say when Bri headed out, except Dad never called Bri "honey."

I no longer need to step into his shoes to earn their respect. Anyway, they won't fit, and I prefer my own.

DISCUSSION QUESTIONS

Whether you're teaching a class, hosting a book club, or chairing a support group, please use these questions as discussion starters.

Pick and choose what's right for you and feel free to add your own questions. If your students come up with additional questions, feel free to share the good ones and I'll add them to my author website, www. blynngoodwin.com.

Why do you think Sandee spells her name non-traditionally? How is it working for her?

Will Sandee and Diego stay a couple? Why or why not? Extra Credit: What are the elements of a lasting relationship or friendship?

What do you look for in a good friend? Are you like or unlike Sandee?

If you could ask three questions of any one character, what would they be? Once you have identified the character and written the questions, trade papers with a partner. Answer the questions the way you think the character would. Then answer them as yourself.

Describe Sandee from the point of view of any other character. Speak in that character's voice. If you write it on the computer, pick their color of ink and their favorite font.

How does the interaction between the sexes compare to your own experience?

Where do Sandee's dreams come from? Do they predict anything or are they created by worry? Explain.

Does your high school have a theater? How does it compare to the one in *Talent*?

How is your school like and unlike the one described in *Talent*?

Which teacher in your school is most like Ms. G? What do they have in common?

Research the support groups that exist for the families of soldiers. How do you think these groups help a family?

How does war change the family of a soldier? If you have a soldier in your family, include your personal experience.

How does the author handle bringing prop guns on campus? Is this realistic? Why or why not?

Who do you know that is like Sandee, Diego, Rob, Jenn, Nicole, Tessa? What do they have in common?

What does the cover tell you about the book? How would you illustrate the cover?

Is the book realistic? Why or why not?

Imagine that this book becomes a movie and you are the casting director. Who would you cast as Sandee, Diego, Rob, Jenn, Nicole, Tessa, and Ms. G? Give one reason for each choice. Do not repeat a reason.

Make two lists: What is within Sandee's control? What is beyond her control? Why is it important to have a blend of both in any novel?

What does this book tell you about how the world works and how high school works? (Extra Credit if you get answers from three other readers and compare their answers to your own.)

If you had a chance to change the title, would you? If so, what would you call this story?

What could an adult in a position of power learn from this book?

What could a parent learn from this book?

What could a teacher or school administrator learn from this book?

What do you think Sandee will do with her newly discovered talents?

What one question would you like to ask the author? Extra Credit: See if you can contact her. Be sure to tell her why you are writing. If she sends you an answer, share it with the class. Please keep it to one question since authors are busy people.

CPSIA information can be obtained
at www.ICGtesting.com
Printed in the USA
FSHW012314200921
84817FS